The Art
of
Salvation

A message for her: the quiet, *abused*, and abandoned

By:

Brittany "Queen Freedom" Williams

www.queenfreedom.com

An imprint of Through Words Publishing House, LLC
Severn, MD

First print book edition: 2016

The publisher is not responsible for websites (or their content) mentioned in this book that are not owned by the publisher.

ISBN-13: 978-0692683842

Acknowledgements

First, I want to thank God for giving me the vision to write this book. He gave it to me in a dream which was very short but detailed. In the dream, the scenery was the beautiful blue bright sky and the clouds were white and fluffy. Out of the blue the phrase "The Art of Salvation" appeared on top of a cloud. It was only a one minute dream. I didn't know what God wanted me to know at the time, but when I woke up I wrote that phrase down because I knew I needed to remember it. Sometime after, I wrote a poem with the same title and God has now allowed me to turn it into a book.

My favorite scripture is Psalm 139:14 which says, "I praise thee that I am fearfully and wonderfully made, marvelous are thy works and my soul knoweth right well". For a long time I would recite that scripture to get me through inner battles. Now I recite this scripture because I know that God has created a beautiful soul within me and it's time to share it with the world.

I also want to thank God for giving me my mother. She is an awesome strong woman who has taught me so much about stepping up to the plate when need be. I've learned from her that life won't always go as planned but when you stand up and take control over your situation everything will work out for the good.

I want to thank my pastors old and new, church family and ministry friends, and all supporters who have supported me throughout this journey. You all have prayed with me, encouraged me, and been the spiritual examples I needed to overcome extreme obstacles. I love you all and I thank you from the bottom of my heart.

To the remainder of my family, who I love dearly and who have always supported me throughout my life, I want to thank you all for being there when it counts and never giving up on me.

Lastly, I want to thank my sister for loving me in spite of the imperfect life I chose before Christ. You have seen me transition from an immature little girl and blossom into a strong young woman. I love you with all my heart, you are more than a sister, and I'll do anything to see you shine. "The Art of Salvation" is dedicated to you because you are at that age where you will experience many stumbling blocks, so I'm honored to be that role model now that I wasn't then and to walk you through life as best as I know how, through Christ.

Message for HER

Hello Queen,

My name is Brittany also known as Queen Freedom. I am a domestic violence and child sex abuse survivor, a former pornography and sex addict and a proud Christian. As a female you should know that identity and character is everything, so I admit this because you need to know who I was and why I am who I have become today. I don't have a degree or a certificate but I am the living witness of God's grace and that is why I am qualified to write this book. I'm open about my past because it is someone's present and will be a person's future if they don't get help now. I've gotten a lot of opposition about my honesty but if it will save a life then I will continue to speak.

As a young woman I have experienced countless failures, triumphs, and victories but no one explains in detail the excessive torment the mind goes through during these times, so God had me write through those experiences. I can't guarantee my story is the answer to every situation, but the only way I pushed through is with God's Word, protection, patience, unconditional love, and a small mustard seed of faith. I realized I had to be ok with knowing that I am beautifully imperfect. I was ashamed of my past and never wanted anyone to know my skeletons then and now, but God had a different plan. He sent me through to build tough skin in this world and to tell someone else that they are never alone.

I always tried to find the answers to my problems or to put the broken pieces together. With an independent mindset I didn't think anyone had the answers but me. When an individual is hurt so many times they stop giving people permission to handle the feelings that others stepped on. This is what I did. I closed my true feelings and only let people see what I wanted them to see. As time went on God opened those bottled emotions and I had to deal with them all one by one. It's funny how He works because I didn't care about Him when I was younger. I was cold hearted and selfish because, as triumph after triumph elevated in my life, I felt it was no way there was a "God". As you continue to read my story you will understand why after almost giving up I can still say, "I love God, He is real, and He is a healer."

God Bless

Part 1:

And so it Begins

Psalm 139:14
I praise thee that I am fearfully and wonderfully made
Marvelous are thy works and my soul knoweth right well

I could feel it in the air that something bad was about to happen. I knew my family was being ripped apart but I didn't know why. With the excessive amount of happiness I consumed as a child, I couldn't seem to figure out why my parents argued so much, but they did. I'm grateful my sister didn't see or hear what I experienced because it was as if my happy spoiled life turned to tragedy and turmoil fast.

And so it begins:

I was sitting at the dinner table doing my homework and I heard loud tumbling above me. I looked and it was my father running down the steps with my mother's purse and my mother running after him. For whatever reason my mom didn't want to give him any money so he was trying to take it himself out of her purse. It got so heavily intense that they went from the stairs, tussled passed me, went through the kitchen, and ended up on top of the basement stairs where they continued to argue. Adrenaline started to rush through my body that I uncontrollably yelled, "LEAVE MY MOMMY ALONE." My dad turned around, got in my face, and said, "WHO ARE YOU TALKING TO!!!" I was so terrified that I couldn't speak. I just turned around to the table, as my body started to tremble, and continued my homework. Shortly after everything eventually calmed down my father said to me, "I will never hit your mother." I heard his words but I didn't believe them. He must have saw the disbelief on my face as well because he asked my mother to reassure me of what he just said but instead my mother replied, "You're so big and bad why don't you tell her yourself." My mind, body, and soul consumed a lot of frustration from continuous arguing. I didn't know the level of rage I could hold in my small body which haunted me over half of my life. I couldn't handle the sound of anger, intense arguing from my parents, and loud banging. It was so much noise that it tormented my ears and I just didn't know what to do.

I would ask God, "What happened to my perfect life"?
Attending Catholic Church allowed me to learn so much about
how Jesus died on the cross for us, how He would answer our
prayers, and how we will suffer no more because we follow
Christ. I just didn't understand why my life was heading this
way when I learned the opposite. My father never went to
church with us and the times we did go was when my sister
and I sang in the choir. I had no relationship with Jesus but I
loved to sing and that's what kept us in church. When we got
home it was a different story. At the age of six, I would cry
about the good ole days because I wanted them to come back. I
felt sorry for my mother because that was not a battle she
asked for and furthermore she couldn't win. I wasn't big
enough to protect my mother which made me feel helpless. To
my knowledge, my father never physically abused my mother
but I can only imagine the emotional and mental abuse couldn't
have been any less painful. Days that I couldn't take the
arguing I would either write about my feelings, go outside to
play, or visit a friend but I didn't realize leaving the flames only
lead me straight to the fire.

Tales of the Fondler

There once was a Fondler who lived in poverty
Dysfunctional home and heart filled with vacancy
Although big as Goliath and very intimidating
The victim wasn't ready for this awakening

"Come over" says the Fondler, "We will watch some movies"
The young girl didn't hesitate and said "ABSOLUTELY"
They were good friends so nothing seemed unmoral
Until the movie they watched appeared to be porno

"What is this" the young girl asked
The Fondler replied with a dark laugh
"This is what I want done to me"
"Look, watch, imitate everything"

"Ew No" the young girl replied
"Get off me, I won't comply"
The Fondler kissed spots never felt before
The young girl's in a trance and wanting more

The Fondler guided the young girl's hand
To feel on places she thought were banned
The Fondler proceeds to instruct the girl
To lick around in a circle

At the age of six the young girl experienced
Her innocence stripped with new experiences
At the age of 7 The Fondler was penetrated
The demon of lust was now activated

Funny it seems how the cycle goes
When children repeat what they quietly know
This happened from the age of 6 to 13

She didn't say a word, all she knew was secrecy

Tales of the Fondler
That walks so quietly
Who was the Fondler
The Fondler was she

Yes, it happened. I was molested. For identity purposes I'll call her Susie. Susie was 7 and I was 6 years old. She was not a normal seven year old because she was much taller than I was. She was my friend but her size and demeanor scared me. Susie and I played together, hung out together, and all of our friends including us were even on the same basketball team. I would not have seen this coming a mile away because I was too young to fully know what was going on at first but I knew I couldn't stop her. The words sex, molestation, etc... were not in my vocabulary at 6 so after continuous back and forth convincing I just gave in and went with the flow.

I was a timid little girl who didn't fight at all so that option was out. I remember it so clearly. I went over Susie's house, like any other time I would leave home from my parents arguing, and we went in the basement to watch movies. I thought this was normal because watching movies is what friends do. She put in a tape and I remember seeing naked bodies, kissing, and caressing. Susie started to kiss and feel on me to get me aroused. Once she knew I was at that point she said, "I want to try what they're doing" and so we did. My body was frozen and I just let it go on. It was almost as if she was either a professional or a professional imitator because it seemed like she really knew what she was doing.

After this offense I felt so disgusting and tried to wrap my head around what happened. I would ask myself how did I get here, how did I let this happen, do I tell my parents, do I stop being her friend, do other people do this, is she doing this to our other friends? I borderline blamed myself at first because I didn't stop her. I had so many questions but I stored all of my feelings inside and kept my mouth shut because through those questions there was something in my mind that wanted to keep going back. The feelings I felt through each action we committed was like a new satisfaction that I realized I wanted to keep, so this went on for 7 years until I was 13.

I can honestly say as time went on I grew attraction to this act. This was the start of my sex addiction. It felt so good to my body and it was like she knew the perfect spots to caress for me to want more. When we were together my mind shut off any anger I had from home situations and in that moment it was as if I was free from all the hurt and pain. In that moment I felt like I was in control. I wasn't attracted to her or even females and I never molested anyone like she did me, but I was attracted to the sexual feeling we both experienced. Sickening right? No. It wasn't sick to a person who never felt any of those feelings before and knowing that it was filling the emptiness inside of me made it ok.

My home was tearing apart and I was so young that I couldn't control my own life so that act, even though sickening, was my control because I knew she would keep calling me to come. I felt wanted and she gave me attention. My mother was so busy taking care of the household and keeping her sanity that emotionally I wasn't connected to anybody. My mother is the type of person that does not like her business in the hands of another person so secrecy was embedded in me very young. With that being said I didn't say anything about Susie because it was a routine for me not to speak. I didn't speak about anything which is probably why my mother would always sneak and read my diaries. I would get so angry at her because my privacy was important to me and I felt that if we are silent as a household then it's no need for me to speak about what I wrote.

Susie became my release for all of the emotional baggage that I carried. It went from molestation to a regularly sexual relationship. It became normal to me. I had other friends I could run to when it got too crazy in the household but as crazy as it sounds I was already sexually attached to Susie and the first person that came to mind when I left my house's dysfunction was her. Through Susie I learned certain body parts reactions and what I needed to do to myself to climax. Masturbation was a part of my life very early and it is something I wish I never learned. That form of lust is something that's difficult to escape because it's not being performed by another person. It's only you. I would do it when I was with her and even when I was bored at home. I had an addiction to this. Even if I didn't feel pleasure it was still done.

Being a creative person I even used different ways to masturbate including small toys or anything that vibrates, pornography, and even the water pressure from the shower head. Yes, you read the previous sentence correct. The mind is filled with so much imagination that a thought can turn into real life, especially if you're a visionary or a visual learner with lust on the brain. This means if you have a lustful mind then you will act on it because your mind knows how to paint picture's so well for you to actually want to do it. When you're addicted to something your mind does not care about the pleasure but about the want and my body wanted it. You might think to yourself, "How can one be addicted to masturbation"? Well, does your body urge for it? Is the climax moment something your mind continues to think about? When conducting in this act do you try to see if you can reach that moment before someone catches you, sort of like a sexual game? Do you hide it or only talk about it to "certain people"? This means you only talk to people who are like you but to other people you don't speak about it because you know the difference between right and wrong in your subconscious. Do you watch pornography to get you aroused so you can masturbate, to learn how to do it better, or to pleasure yourself with it after your weren't fully satisfied by your partner? When you're masturbating do you visualize those pornographic images to heighten your climax moment? Do you require or expect this in your relationship or marriage and if it doesn't happen are you in a bad mood? Do you often feel sporadic urges in your vagina that reminds you of it? Are you upset, actually borderline severely frustrated, if that climax moment isn't what your mind said it would be? Most of all, do you masturbate because your life might be out of control and in your mind this act is the only thing you have left. If all or most of the answers to these questions is a yes then that my friend is an addiction and it is taking over your life. A lot of people don't see self-pleasure as a sin but treating the body as a sex doll for a temporary fix is very degrading to you and disappointing to God. You are sexually admiring what masturbation can do for you for a moment but in the end it does nothing but destroy your insides spiritually. I know this because in the New Testament in Romans chapter 8 verses 16-17 it states: *The Spirit Himself bears witness with our spirit that we are children of God, and if children, then heirs-heirs of God and joint heirs with Christ, if indeed we suffer with Him, that we may also be glorified together.*

This means that since we are joint heirs with Christ then He is feeling everything we feel. This includes the money, food, sex, drugs, etc. Whatever we have an addiction to Christ feels the self-abuse with you. We have to pay attention to what is slowly trying to control our lives so we can take that control back.

As you've read in the poem, *"Tales of the Fondler"*, Susie taught me how to pleasure her with my tongue, my fingers, and I learned sexual languages and low sexual tones to use to turn her on. I learned all of this so young and I carried that with me towards myself and into adulthood. All of this knowledge played a part in the pictures my mind painted which caused me to go to this for healing. Susie and everything we did was my god. Masturbation was my cure for pleasure, boredom, anger, a release from stress, and an act that filled time until the next time I saw Susie. She was almost like my teacher without even knowing.

USA Today states, "Rarely mentioned is the sobering statistic that more than one-third of the sexual abuse of America's children is committed by other minors." I do not blame my mother and father for what happened to me but I want parents to know when your child is out of your sight things like this can happen. My advice is to be as open with communication about real life as possible, pray with your child and share Jesus with them, and most of all pay attention to your child's emotions. Don't let them shut you out. I can guarantee something is being bottled up inside of that little body and you don't want it to be too late where communication is nonexistent. (*Parents this means that it can happen to your child and because there is so much secrecy in the household they don't know that it's wrong. They might think of it as a game or as I did new satisfaction, so please be open with your child and at least minimum teach them the do's and don'ts of how people are supposed to act towards them.*)

When Satan has an agenda there is no gender involved and he doesn't care about who gets hurt in the end which is why I wasn't attracted to Susie but just the act. The more my parents argued the more I was over there and the more Satan used two little girls to destroy each other spiritually. In my immature mind I didn't have much logic or wisdom then but now I realize that she was probably imitating what has happened to her or had seen more than once. When we are victims of drastic acts we don't care too much about our attackers reasoning but about how we feel. It takes a lot of healing to understand their actions towards us wasn't intentional no matter how perverted. This perversion reminds me of a couple of books in the Old Testament of the bible where God speaks about same sex acts and more. The first scripture is from the book of Genesis where Lot, Abraham's nephew, was in Sodom where there was a lot of wickedness in the land. Two angels made their way there to destroy the city where they found Lot. He was hesitant for the angels to enter the city because he knew of the wickedness and perversion taking place. Lot was afraid if anyone saw them then the men

16

of the city would have their way with them. These people were molesters, pedophiles, rapists, etc. and God had enough of it. The men of the city somehow found out and were furious about the angels stay and wanted to sexually harm them. They tried to break down Lot's door but he stood in between the people and the door and this is what they said:

> *Genesis 19:5 "And they called to Lot and said to him, "Where are the men who came to you tonight? Bring them out to us that we may know them carnally (meaning to pleasure their flesh with the angels)"*

> *Genesis 19:9 "And they said, "Stand back!" Then they said, "This one (meaning Lot) came in to stay here, and he keeps acting as a judge; now we will deal worse with you than with them." So they pressed hard against the man Lot, and came near to break down the door.*

The second scripture is from the book of Leviticus where God instructed Moses to guide the people of Israel out of Egypt. He gave Moses a set of commandments that the people of Israel needed to obey and this was one of them:

> *Leviticus 20:13 "If a man lies with a male as he lies with a woman, both of them have committed an abomination. They shall surely be put to death. Their blood shall be upon them."*

God would not have given these people this commandment or destroyed the city of Sodom if same sex acts weren't taking place. Sad to say but it is still happening now. I was in the same midst of these acts with Susie which means God's Word is still relevant from all those years ago. Understand this, I will never put one sin above another or single one sin out but in any situation that has caused me pain the devil has always been involved.

To the queen reading this who has been in my situation, please talk to someone and don't let your emotions build so high that you lose control of the only body God made specifically for you. The reason I kept going back to Susie is because I didn't know the spirit of lust and masturbation had a hold of me. If I would've said something it could've been a different story. Understand this, Satan has the ability to possess, oppress, depress, and suppress anyone young and old to do what he wants. Don't be ashamed of anything you've been through or have even administered yourself. What I mean is an oppressed or depressed person, especially female, will fill emptiness any way they know how including sex, drugs, etc. If you have conducted these acts don't beat yourself up over it because Satan has the cunning nature to make you do things you normally wouldn't do but make you think it was your fault. Realize who is really in control and if you don't take your control back Satan will continue to use you for his good and humiliate you for filth. He preys on people who are vulnerable and disguises himself to look like something or someone you need. The reason why you can't get that person out of your head after you have a sexual encounter with them is because the devil plays with the mind and taunts it to his liking. That knight and shining armor turned out to be a dog because you didn't see or ignored the signs at hand.

The only way to defeat Satan is prayer, wanting to change your ways, and surrounding yourself with positivity and with people who know how to pray. What prayer does is counters Satan's attacks and torment. It is words from God that pushes the devil away from you. I understand that everyone who reads this book possibly does not believe in God and has questions about the bible, but one thing you don't need to question is the power of God's Word and the mighty weapon it holds against Satan. The only way you don't believe in God's Word is if you want to be the devils friend (or minion).

Scriptures for Protection

*Psalm 23

The LORD is my shepherd;
I shall not want.
He makes me to lie down in green pastures;
He leads me beside the still waters.
He restores my soul;
He leads me in the paths of righteousness
For His name's sake.
Yea, though I walk through the valley of the
shadow of death,
I will fear no evil;
For You are with me;
Your rod and Your staff, they comfort me.
You prepare a table before me in the
presence of my enemies;
You anoint my head with oil;
My cup runs over.
Surely goodness and mercy shall follow me
All the days of my life;
And I will dwell in the house of the LORD
Forever.

*Psalm 91

He who dwells in the secret place of the Most High
Shall abide under the shadow of the Almighty.
I will say of the LORD, "He is my refuge and my fortress;
My God, in Him I will trust."
Surely He shall deliver you from the snare of the fowler[a]
And from the perilous pestilence.
He shall cover you with His feathers,
And under His wings you shall take refuge;
His truth shall be your shield and buckler.

You shall not be afraid of the terror by night,
Nor of the arrow that flies by day,
Nor of the pestilence that walks in darkness,
Nor of the destruction that lays waste at noonday.
A thousand may fall at your side,
And ten thousand at your right hand;
But it shall not come near you.
Only with your eyes shall you look,
And see the reward of the wicked.
Because you have made the LORD, who is my refuge,
Even the Most High, your dwelling place,
10 No evil shall befall you,
Nor shall any plague come near your dwelling;
For He shall give His angels charge over you,
To keep you in all your ways.
In their hands they shall bear you up,
Lest you dash your foot against a stone.
You shall tread upon the lion and the cobra,
The young lion and the serpent
you shall trample underfoot.
"Because he has set his love upon me,
therefore I will deliver him;
I will set him on high, because he has known My name.
He shall call upon Me, and I will answer him;
I will be with him in trouble;
I will deliver him and honor him.
With long life I will satisfy him,
And show him My salvation."

Ephesians 6: 10-20

Finally, my brethren, be strong in the Lord and in the power of His might. Put on the whole armor of God that you may be able to stand against the wiles of the devil. For we do not wrestle against flesh and blood, but against principalities, against powers, against the rulers of the darkness of this age, against spiritual hosts of wickedness in the heavenly places. Therefore take up the whole armor of God

that you may be able to withstand in the evil day, and having done all, to stand.
Stand therefore, having girded your waist with truth, having put on the breastplate of righteousness, and having shod your feet with the preparation of the gospel of peace; above all, taking the shield of faith with which you will be able to quench all the fiery darts of the wicked one. And take the helmet of salvation, and the sword of the Spirit, which is the word of God; praying always with all prayer and supplication in the Spirit, being watchful to this end with all perseverance and supplication for all the saints and for me, that utterance may be given to me, that I may open my mouth boldly to make known the mystery of the gospel, for which I am an ambassador in chains; that in it I may speak boldly, as I ought to speak.

Psalm 139:14
I will praise You, for I am fearfully and wonderfully made;
Marvelous are Your works,
And that my soul knows very well.

1 Peter 2:9-10
But you are a chosen generation, a royal priesthood, a holy nation, His own special people, that you may proclaim the praises of Him who called you out of darkness into His marvelous light; who once were not a people but are now the people of God, who had not obtained mercy but now have obtained mercy

When you continuously read the Bible and don't give the devil any room to haunt you, that's how you know that God's Word holds true to what it says. The only way it won't is if you're not consistent. You can't be an on and off person because inconsistency confuses your spirit and gives the devil space to creep in. Being consistent gives him no space at all. These scriptures are simply Gods protection for your spirit so the devil can't get to it. Please understand there are many more but you have to read the bible for yourself to know them.

A message to Susie

Even though we were kids, for a long time I blamed you for molesting me. I was mad at you for taking advantage of my timid nature and for not protecting me. I felt like everything you did was on purpose and you had a motive. My anger for you grew so rapidly that I vowed to never speak to you again. Now that I am older I see what actually happened behind the scenes and I'm aware of Satan's antics. It's not your fault and I forgive you. I'm no longer bound by this act, or even lust, and I can live my life in freedom. I hope that you are living in peace and understand that we may never speak but know that I love you not because I have to but because I choose to. You are a great person who chose to act in an outer body way. As I said I forgive you and love you.

I'm free

Britt

My Dad

Throughout the seven years of sexual activity with Susie my body was temporarily satisfied but became so numb and used up. I was happy on the outside but dying on the inside. I had nothing to lean on while going through all of these acts with Susie which left me spiritually dead. What is even crazier is that I was good at hiding it. To a child that young, it takes a certain level of skill to build that and I did. The only way I was able to stay partially sane was writing. I wrote about everything including my father.

How could you leave me?
12/15/2008

HOW COULD YOU LEAVE ME?!!!
YOU WON'T EVER SEE ME GROW
YOU WON'T EVER SEE ME DEVELOP INTO WOMANHOOD
BUT IT'S NOT AS IF YOU SHOULD BECAUSE YOU NEVER COULD

YOU IGNORED EVERY OPPORTUNITY NOT CARING ABOUT MY GOODS
HOW COULD YOU LEAVE ME?
HOW COULD YOU LEAVE YOUR FIRST BORN?
DADDY'S LITTLE GIRL WHO ALWAYS RAN INTO YOUR ARMS
TO ACT AS IF YOU DON'T KNOW ME NOT EVEN A PHONE CALL

BUT YOU HAVE THE REPUTATION OF A GOOD MAN
EVERY LITTLE KIDS ROLE MODEL BUT FUCKED US OVER FULL THROTTLE
HOW COULD YOU LEAVE ME?
WHY WOULD YOU LEAVE US?
YOUR FAMILY THAT YOU CLAIM YOU LOVED
WHO KNOWS WHY
HONESTLY I DON'T WANT TO KNOW THE TRUTH

I LOVE YOU BUT I WISH I WOULD'VE HEARD THE LOVE FROM YOU
HOPEFULLY WE'LL MEET AGAIN WHEN I GET TO HEAVEN
HOW COULD YOU LEAVE ME?
BEEN ASKING THAT QUESTION SINCE TEN
HOW?

My father was a funny man. He was always laughing and his jokes had the whole room on the floor. I was a daddy's girl. I loved his presence and knowing that I was safe meant a lot to me. He had this specific laugh that made me smile because it showed so much joy in his face. I remember his smile so distinctly because he had a chipped tooth in the front but that didn't stop him from smiling. I would ask him how did his tooth get this way and he would joke and say, "Your mother did it." I have that joking trait in me as well. Anytime I smile someone else smile's with me. I love my dad.

Unfortunately, I wasn't able to experience him for long because I was about 10 years old when he left. It's funny because my instinct knew it was eventually coming after being around anger for so long. I remember my father would do weird things that didn't seem normal and I saw that my mother had enough. He would let people borrow the tags from my mother's car, leave me in the car when he would visit his friends, and forget to pick my sister and me up after school sometimes. I even witnessed him get arrested. We were on our way home and we stopped in front of a house on the hill before our street. He kept looking up at the house like he was trying to watch someone or figure out what those people were doing. I remember saying," Daddy why are we stopping, our house is right there." He said, "I'm just looking for something, we will be home in a minute." We sat for a few minutes and next thing I knew there was loud banging from a cop on the door for my father to get out the car. I was crying hysterically because I was totally confused. I remember screaming, "NO DON'T TAKE MY DADDY, NO STOP IT!" The officer rudely said, "Oh stop crying little girl, your father will be fine." My dad told me to run to my neighbor's house to call my mom and tell her what happened. Until this day I'm not sure why he got arrested but I do know my mother was fed up. Not long after, our complete family turned into just us girls, the three amigos. We had to adjust but we were fine with the change for a while but something happened that turned my world upset down.

Diary Entry 02/26/2005
I wish I could have an angel to take the place of me. To go through the pain I went through when my daddy got up to leave. Experience the tears and the fears that I fear. Then I can be free from the hard times around me. To hear the gunshots and one day that could be me. So I need an angel to set my soul free.

"I just had a dream where I saw a figure of my father. It was his face but it wasn't his actions, it's like he was possessed. He was speaking in a high voice and moving in a weird way. At first I said what's wrong what's wrong. But then spiritually I realized I needed to cast the demon out of him that took possession of his body so I started to say, "In the name of Jesus get out of my daddy Satan. I cast you out of him in the name of Jesus. Flee from him!!!" I repeated this over and over. I realized it wasn't working so I grabbed my father's head extremely tight and started casting out again. I'm not sure if it left but I started crying not long after and then I woke up."

I came in the house one night after work and my mother broke the news to my sister and me that my father was dead. I was in high school at this time. I ran to my room and broke into tears. As usual, I hid my emotions in my room and I didn't want to be consoled or even speak. At this time we moved into a new house so I hadn't spoken to or seen my father in about a year and a half. I understood the reason was because he moved back to his hometown. As a result my sister and I hardly saw him but surprisingly one day my mother called me and said, "Your father wants to see you and your sister." I was the happiest girl in the world because, despite of all the hatred I had for him, I was still a daddy's girl. He came to my grandmother's house and I gave him the biggest hug. He gave my sister and I a card that had 100 dollars in it. I can't lie and say I wasn't excited about the money but I was even happier that he was there after so long. On the other hand, my father didn't look like himself. He was so skinny and his face was as long as a banana. I remembered him being healthy with a round face like me but I didn't question it. We had a good time that day.

In fact I remember my sister and me quizzing my father to see if he still knew things about us like our birthday, where we were born, our middle name, etc. I think my sister was treating it as a game but inside I really wanted to know if he knew all of those things about me just to see if he still cared. Surprisingly he got all of those answers right and I was left feeling better that, in spite of his appearance, he was still the same man that I once knew and loved. After that day I didn't realize that was the last time I would see him.

My father died on Labor Day of 2008 and I remember the funeral like it was yesterday. I sat in the front pew of the church with my mother and sister and didn't shed one tear. I felt like how could I cry for someone who emotionally and physically abandoned me and now I permanently won't get the opportunity to speak to him again. I felt robbed. I listened to everyone speak so highly of my father and how much the kids looked up to him. He was also a part of a fraternity so his frat brothers spoke highly of him as well. I was CONFUSED but understanding of these descriptions because that was the man I knew in my earlier years but the man I grew to hate was the total opposite. I felt he didn't do his job as a man when it counted. He didn't teach me about the male gender, the heart aches, the mind games, the urges, the confusion, etc. I learned all of that on my own which unfortunately is the reason for most of my scars.

As you saw in my dream he had no control over his mind, body, or anger but as a child I would not have understood that. I couldn't understand the state he was in and probably didn't want to hear anything negative about him. I am occasionally tormented by my father's death. What I mean is sometimes I get dreams about him and knowing he has died either brings back anger, hurt, or sadness because I do miss him. I can't deny the good memories we shared when I was younger. I just wish this part of my story didn't have to end this way but it did. I'm not sure how my father died but the rumor was he collapsed in the shower. Either way he was gone. I couldn't get him back.

Furthermore, rage and anger progressed throughout my body the day of the funeral and I was so glad it was over. I was the exact definition of a girl with daddy and abandonment issues which showed in my posture that day. I didn't crack a smile and was disinterested in being there. My aunt even said, "Smile Brittany" which I did for a second for her but I went back to myself quick.

I often look back at the family structure I came from and I'm reminded of how blessed I truly am but it's hard as a female to surpass emptiness when every time I looked up there was something new that added to the anger inside of me. First my parents are arguing so angrily that I never want to be home, Susie and I are sex buddies because of it, and now my father is dead. I couldn't take any more pain. In addition, at the time of my father's death I was in a relationship. I was so emotionally weak that I leaned on this person for support, love, and comfort. I later realized that two people with similar hurt should not be together but after the death of my father I felt that that relationship was all I had.

Diary Entry (lost date) 2008
"I just saw a man that looks like my father at work. The way he walked was like he was leaning to the left trying to hold himself up. It was almost like a replica of the characters from "Men in

Black" when the aliens were operating inside the humans and the human body would move in a weird way. I got so emotional because my father is dead and maybe he is checking on me."

A message to my dad

For a long time I despised you because it hurt me when you left. I wrote you off in my mind because I didn't understand how you could just leave us like that. One day my life was just fine and then all of a sudden it came crashing down. I needed you, I cried for you, and I longed for you until my soft heart turned to a cold one. Your face became a distant memory because for a long time I forgot what you looked like. I understand that you were operating with some things that were not of God and in order for us to be safe you had to leave. I also know that God brought you into my life to have a testimony to give. I can now speak to girls who feel abandoned, unloved, unprotected, and confused about why their father was not around and I can tell them that it's all in God's plan. It hurts now but it is only making you stronger because when you get pass it and look back at the pain you had, you will see that you are stronger then you thought you were. It's all in God's divine plan for your life. I've gone through the healing process to forgive you dad and I can say that it wasn't easy but my tears has turned to joy knowing that God put my earthly dad here to give glory to my heavenly father with a testimony like mine. You were supposed to be imperfect because you are human like me and I can do nothing but celebrate the good you did do and rejoice with you when I get to heaven. I love you and forgive you dad.

I'm free

Britt

LIFE LESSONS FROM PART 1

- I kept my mouth shut
- Let myself continue to get violated
- Let my father's absence change my view of him
- Let anger build within me when the situation was uncontrollable
- Try to be in control of myself instead of letting my parents do their job

I know that I was young at the time and I wouldn't have known to do the points above but now I'm older and I can look back and see what I did wrong so you can know. Young lady understood that even if you don't feel in control you really are. You are stronger then you know because just speaking about what you feel gives the enemy less control over you. As you start to expose those deep inner feelings it allows you to slowly break the chains from over your heart. Bondage is not fun especially when it separates you from your parents or the ones who love you. You'll feel alone and will begin to let desperation and emptiness take over. Speak and the chains will break.

Parents when you argue in front of or around your kids it is a sound that sticks with them. It's a mental torment. Every time they hear yelling or loud noise it takes them back to those arguments they heard as a child. This can affect friendships, relationships, jobs, etc. because they won't know how to communicate well. They've only heard you yell so they will do the same

Part 2:

The Abuse

Psalm 139:14
I praise thee that I am fearfully and
wonderfully made
Marvelous are thy works and my soul
knoweth right well

Just had a dream that my abuser shot and tried to kill me. I walked in the house and his best friend and other people were there. I said hello and no one spoke so I turned around and said HELLO can anybody speak back. If I came in y'all house and didn't speak it would be a problem right. So they finally spoke then I walked in the back of house. My abuser comes after me and starts arguing with me saying mean things. I tried to talk to him and calm him down but he gets even angrier. He pulls his gun out and says, "DON'T MAKE ME USE THIS ON YOU". I grabbed the gun out of his hand so he could calm down. His best friend came to the back trying to break it up and after things falsely calmed down I gave the gun back then he shot me. In the dream blood rushed up very fast as if I was dying but I woke up just in time. Felt like I was about to suffocate.

Diary Entry (lost date)
"This bought back so many memories which still haunt me until this day. From the punches, bruises, name calling, and emotional torment sometimes it plays back in my mind. Thoughts of his angry voice show up in my dreams but have the face of people I love...scary"

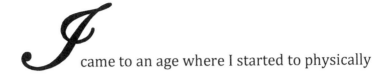 came to an age where I started to physically develop so I was getting a lot of attention from the opposite sex. This was a little weird because as you know my only physical encounter was with Susie and masturbation. I had a chip on my shoulder, as most teens do, and as some would say I was feeling myself. I went on a sexual rampage and became available to the male gender which is common now at this age. What I mean is I gave my virginity away at the age of 15 years old. Boys were now the substitute that filled the emptiness I had within me. I loved sex. It was like a cool new hobby that I eventually mastered.

Being a plus size girl, I was self-conscious about my body because most girls my age were skinny or curvy. Males would compliment that kind of girl so much that when they showered me with endless compliments I would return the favor with my body. At the time I felt my body was the only thing that had any value to give. I didn't feel pretty or heard those fulfilling words from my parents, so males complimenting my body were the words I believed to be true. I was never told why certain parts of my body were to be sacred or kept except from church which I ignored. I liked the way my mind felt when I heard the males speak to me so I definitely wasn't going to tell them to stop. It was almost like a stimulate that cured any insecurities I had.

All of this new love I received created a world wind of emotions. I like this one, I don't like this one, this one is too nice, this one I will sleep with, this one I won't, it was like I had options and I never had that before. I was feeling myself so much that I became a female "player". I always juggled at least about three boys at a time and that's the least. My memory was sharper back then so I could keep up with the lies I told to each of them. I don't know where this sexual vindictive cunning person came from but I felt like why not find a lane that I could be happy. So I became that male magnet without even trying. I took what I learned from Susie and found a way to switch it to play males. I taught males how to engage in phone sex after I learned. This creates a stimulant that gave them a mental fantasy without me being there. Here is where I used the voices that Susie taught me. Over the phone, I played the role of many characters that manipulated the male to visualize the scene as if I was there. Sort of like pornography over the phone.

After I gave my virginity, I didn't care about a STD's, which I did end up getting Chlamydia, or getting pregnant. I started off using condoms but can definitely say I didn't at times as well. My only focus was me and I did what made me happy. I was living the life but one day someone caught my eye and my feelings got involved, which turned into what I thought was true love.

As the end of Part 1 stated I was in a relationship when my father died. I'm going to call him Peter. I met Peter in a summer program where we got a stipend every week for working in a computer setting at an elementary school. I never really noticed him in our work space but one day we crossed paths, had a good conversation after work, exchanged numbers, and began a friendship. It's kind of funny because Peter told me that he told everyone we were together at work before I even knew him. I guess he was a psychic because we talked on the phone all the time and developed feelings for each other very fast. We had different life stories but shared the same hurt from our situations. One evening we made it official and I had a boyfriend.

I wasn't really the relationship type. I would usually just have different guys and let it be over if we didn't speak anymore. Peter was different. I'd never had butterflies for someone so severely before and that's how I knew I was falling in love with him. I hadn't felt that happy since the good memories of my father, so rekindling those feelings definitely caused me to put my all into him. Being with Peter whole heartedly gave me the love back that I'd missed. Whatever he needed I got it or found a way to get it. If he wanted to see me I would make it happen by any means. I didn't care that he was imperfect, had an anger problem, or even disrespected others because, as all females think, I knew he wouldn't get angry with me.

What made our love so beautiful is that he treated me like a queen and anytime I needed to talk he was there. Of course we both didn't have much back then so "treating me like a queen" consisted of his romantic actions towards me and the level of chemistry shared. He treated me like a queen emotionally. I had someone I could spill every emotion to and wasn't judged for it. I finally didn't have to live in secrecy like I did growing up. I mean I could tell him anything and he understood because we shared the same emotion.

I loved him so much that I even went as far as sneaking him in my house at night so he could have somewhere to sleep. He wasn't stable with his living situation so I did what I thought was best. Many can read this and say I was dumb but going from feelings of abandonment to feeling what I thought was total love again was a big deal to me.

The first couple of months of the relationship were awesome. We were an inseparable couple that was attached at the hip. Wherever he went I went and vice versa. Our love was more than a friendship because we shared our deepest passions together. He lied about his age because he was a little younger than me but I didn't care when I found out because the protection and love that he showed me overrode that detail. I was desperate for love before I met him so receiving that meant more to me then Peter's age.

As time went on our chemistry in the relationship started to shift. Reason being is because we had more pain in common than joy. It took a while for our hurt to come out toward each other and it did. A person can only make you happy for so long until your true self is not ok that you have found joy. What I mean is if there is an inner evil in a person it will come forth because it is not ok with the operator being happy. Peter and I were the operators of our own inner evil and it was not happy that we made each other happy. As I stated before I didn't care that he had an anger problem, but that was because it was never personal. Now that the honeymoon stage was over, it became personal. When we argued I was called whores, b**ches, sluts, and many other creative words.

He turned into a completely different person and that rage that I felt when my father left was the same rage I went back to. I wasn't afraid of Peter in the beginning so when we argued my tone would get very rowdy and my smart mouth had an agenda to pierce his weak and vulnerable spots. This is also displayed in my dream on page 32. When we argued I would react like my parents did when I heard them argue, so my mouth was vicious. When our love dimmed, the emptiness I was so desperate to fill had resurfaced. We were both two angry people who, at the time of an argument, weren't afraid to show it.

The first time Peter abused me felt like an outer body experience. We were amongst friends at a bowling alley and the night didn't go so well. We got back to my house and we started arguing about that night. This is what happened. I invited one of my friends to the alley but she needed directions. I stepped outside to clearly hear her on the phone and when I got back inside I saw Peter fuming. He said, "WHERE WERE YOU". I replied, "I went outside to give my friend directions. What's wrong with you." He said, "I WAS LOOKING FOR YOU EVERYWHERE AND I COULDN'T FIND YOU."

Here is where I got upset because I didn't understand why that was such a big deal. I felt that he was not my father and I didn't need to report to him everywhere I go. We were at a place in our relationship where love was still there but we tolerated each other because our chemistry was not completely gone. We were still each other's listening ear and emotional comfort when needed. Our relationship was surviving off of past memories and as that blinded our vision the rage and hate secretly grew.

I can now comprehend that the same protection I loved about Peter is the same protection he had that night at the bowling alley but since the honeymoon stage was over it turned into a heavy possession. It was like I couldn't be out of his sight and it really angered him. Being the person I was I begun to reply with the same tone he had and it turned into a huge blow up. We were in each other's face basically about to scrap like men, the police had to break us up, and unfortunately my friend had to see all of that. I felt like the hulk against Peter because I literally had no fear. It took us a little time to calm down but once we did we were back to loving each other. This is how we were and how we showed we cared.

As I stated before I would sneak him in at night so when we got back to my house, out of the blue, he started speaking about the bowling alley incident again. I thought we were over it but I was mistaken. I viciously replied to what Peter was saying and next thing I know I'm being choked against the couch because it got so heated. I tried to get his hand from around my neck and he eventually let go.

Here is where I began to fear Peter. It's funny because my mindset almost welcomed this act. I'm not saying I wanted him to but my mind wasn't shocked that he choked me. What I mean is this, my mind, body, and soul was attached to Peter so choking me felt like it was just a part of the relationship. It didn't feel wrong but it didn't feel right. I had so much love for him that I accepted his apology and knew how deep his love was for me that it was no way he would do it again. My mind was screwed and I unfortunately identified it as love. Everything was fine for a while but then another "incident" struck. I don't remember what the situation was but I remember being choked so bad that I felt my soul lifting. I literally almost died. He even said he saw my eyes roll in the back of my head which made him let me go. At this point our arguments was more one sided because the fear in me wouldn't allow my words to be as sharp as before. His mind would race with accusations and evilness and the abuse was a result of it. I remember coughing hysterically after he choked me and trying to regain consciousness within my body. Once again he apologized and pleaded with tears sobbing that he was sorry, so I forgave him.

(Parents, especially fathers, if you have a daughter please be the example that she needs. If you are not an example of who she needs to surround herself with then she will do what everyone else is doing or attach herself to emotional connections. The devil has a trap for every person out here and he was able to trip me up because my father fell short in his position. Claim your position as a father and even as a mother and raise your child with knowledge for every aspect of his/her life so that what happened to me won't happen to them.)

We were back to us again and I could see that he was making a change but that didn't last long. 4th of July that year was the day I will never forget. We were with his family celebrating and on that day we decided I didn't want to go back home. I called my mother and told her I wasn't coming back and I was going to live with Peter's family. His mother, two brothers, and two sisters lived in what some would call one of the worst areas to live in but I didn't care, I just wanted to be with him. I know what some of you are thinking. How could you leave your house to move with your boyfriend and his family?

38

I was in love, that's all I can say. It was an addictive attachment and I didn't see myself with anyone else but him. My feelings were so strong for Peter that if he said jump I would've said how high. This ladies, is a classic case of a girl with daddy issues.

Living in the house with his family wasn't that bad at first. They accepted me and invited me in but his mother knew something was up. She must have been psychic because she knew he was hitting me. She started to take up for me and began despising her son which he blamed me for. That house elevated to be hell on wheels. Throughout all of this madness I did have a job but I missed a lot of days because I was with him. Being afraid he would cheat on me, I would stay with him to watch him. It was almost as if I was mentally becoming him. I got fired from that job but thankfully started employment at another one very fast.

I remember one night we were all in the house and his mother started arguing with him about me. He began to get mad because he felt I was turning his mother against him which wasn't true. His actions turned her against him. So I was sitting in the kitchen listening to them argue, his mother angrily walks outside, and next thing I know I get punched in the face. His brothers and sisters started crying so he panicked and drug me out the house because he knew his mother was going to kick him out. I was barefoot walking the street with him and he was fuming with rage. We ended up resting on a stoop and next thing I know there is gunshots very close by so we take off running. We waited a few minutes and eventually we went back to the house so I could get some shoes. We ended up riding the bus until his mother let us back in.

This started to be the turning point that I didn't need to be there but I didn't have the courage to leave. My mother pleaded with me to come home but I didn't budge. She even came to visit me with my grandmother but I didn't go with her. She started crying as if she was losing her daughter and truth be told she was right because I was dying inside but my head was so screwed that I felt I had to stay. My mindset was I'd rather be empty with someone emotionally attached to me then go home where I'm just empty.

The thing is that my mother was always a great mother but we were never able to have those deep conversations where I could really cry to her about my feelings. She is a sweet person but has a hard shell when it comes to real emotions. This disconnect led me to seek whoever would listen to my feelings and the one who happened to stick was Peter. My other family members even tried to get me to come home by picking him and I up to get us out of that environment and talking to us about our actions.

Everything was happening so fast and I was quickly deteriorating before my mother's eyes that she decided to finally tell me the full unclosed story about my father over the phone. On the inside I wanted to know why I felt I had to be attached to Susie when I didn't want to be, why did my father want my mother's purse that day, why he let people borrow the tags from the car, why he forgot to pick my sister and I up from school, why he left me in the car when he went to his friend's house, why they argued disrespectfully, why I tolerate Peter so much, and why after begging and pleading didn't my mother want to answer any questions I had about my father.

So at the age of 18 I finally found out my father was on crack since I was a little girl and he didn't leave us but he went to rehab for treatment. He actually started using when we were living with my grandmother before we moved to our first house. This explains the constant arguments between my parents, the mental abuse my mother endured, and the reason I didn't want to stay home. When she told me about rehab I actually remember visiting him there when I was younger but I didn't know where we were.

It was like everything started to come together in my life and the missing pieces were finally found but honestly I didn't take it well. I had too much information to take in at once and not to mention I was already under heavy darkness being attached to Peter. My face couldn't have been redder. I was fuming with anger. It was so much I didn't know and to think that something as big as this information wasn't explained to me until now while I'm in my darkness was not suitable for my brain. I was mentally dead. My rage for my father was at an all-time high. I hated him all over again. It's sad because my mind was starting to get clear and I was actually considering leaving Peter but with that information I clung to my boyfriend even more.

Time goes on and after constant pleading from my family, eventually I did go home but it didn't last. It was like I couldn't be away from Peter. One night I spoke to him on the phone and he stated he wanted me to be with him where he was. At this time his mother kicked him out so he wasn't living anywhere. He was moving from house to house hoping someone would let him stay. So ask yourself, how was I going to be where he was when he didn't have a home? The answer is simple, we were homeless. I packed a bag and ran out the door. My mother, grandmother, and sister ran after me pleading with me to stay but I kept running.

My family was so hurt but I kept going. I took a train to where he was and there we were two teenagers with nowhere to go. We slept at round trip bus stations, train stations, crack head houses, on the bench in parks, and we even got tattoos of each other's name on us with the little money I had left over. Oh, and if you're wondering the abuse didn't stop. He wasn't a person who constantly beat me but if he is mad enough it is a whole other story. The constant verbal attacks felt like abuse and the fear and love I had for him was a deadly combination. We had no money so he started selling drugs so we could eat. I lost so much weight that summer because we walked everywhere.

There was a time when I thought I was pregnant by him but thank God that wasn't the case. Many cold nights and summer days were the highlight of my life. I remember sleeping all the time and when I woke up I watched people pass by wishing I could be as happy as them. I had no life. Prior to that, I was failing college because I was skipping class to be with him. I was an immature minded runaway, a statistic, and a young and dumb young lady who had nothing to call her own.

After some time, I eventually called my mother to come pick me up because I was ready to come home. My mother didn't have to come when I disrespected her to the core but she did. She is the epitome of a mother who unconditionally loves her child. One would think I learned my lesson and broke up with him but I didn't. I stayed in a relationship but my mind began to become clear again. The last straw was a situation that led me to get arrested which is illustrated in the poem below called, "Cased Dismissed." I wrote this explaining a couple of the domestic events that took place and not just focusing on one story.

Case Dismissed
06/24/2013-06/25/2013

I sit and watch as you pace back and forth conversing with yourself
But yourself is not yourself
So I sit and wait until the anticipation grows near
I feel a squeeze I can't breathe Lord how did I get here
My eyes closed
I feel my soul separate from my frame
He lets go
Nothing but back thoughts in my membrane
Satan is calling my name, so I answered

Feeling anger so viscously from my head to my feet
Feeling it travel through my spirit until its mission is complete
All I hear is murder, murder, use murder to defeat
My eyes are squinting, I'm different, I'm no longer me
I looked over to the knife block
A substitute for what I didn't have for a gunshot
Grabbed the longest one I could find to slice his meat like pork chops
You would've thought it was "Good Fellas" how I wanted to dump his body at a truck stop
But something came over me
And even though I stabbed him it wasn't as deep as his arteries
That goes to show when you're not in control God still covers me
But the plot thickens
Ten days after my birthday I get a knock at the door
"Are you Brittany?"
"Yes"
I get handcuffed and escorted out the door
A 45,000 dollar bail set
Charged with second degree assault and I'm the threat
Could've faced ten years in jail all for squeezing my neck but you couldn't show up in front of the judge when it's time to get cross checked
Look at God still working with me
Because even though I rejected Him He still covered
So before you think the Lord has left you alone in a dark mist
I'm a living testimony
Case Dismissed

We were in my house one day and if you were wondering, yes, I was still sneaking him in at night because he had nowhere to go. One day he woke up and said he wanted to his family's house. This made me upset because I wanted him to be with me. My mindset was if I wasn't in school and had no life, the least he could do was stayed with me and quite frankly that way I knew he wasn't with another girl. He got in the shower and I got in my mother's shower. He was use to me taking showers with him so he got upset at that. I made sure I

43

finished my shower the same time he finished so I couldn't be defenseless and unbalanced by the water if he decided to come attack me. I went in the bathroom where he was and grabbed my face cleanser. When he saw me he said, "What do you want?" I said, "I'm not in here for you." He got frustrated at my smart comment and tried to grab the stringent out of my hand. The stringent splashed in my face and burned my eyes. I ran downstairs to clean them and let me remind you that I was still in my towel during all of this. He came downstairs and found me pouring a cup of juice. He started arguing with me and next thing I know he threw the drink in my face. I go sit in the living room to wipe my face off once again. At this time my mind has so many evil thoughts brewing.

I remember thinking if I go to the closet and get the hammer and hit him with it, I can beat him enough to leave me alone but not go as far as killing him. I'm sure I had other thoughts as well but the main thing I wanted was to stay safe. I went into the kitchen to lean on the sink.

In the heat of the argument he came around to where I was, got in my face, and tried to tackle me. The only thing that held me up was the sink I was leaning on. He proceeded to yell in anger, "I WILL FU***NG KILL YOU." I was so fed up with the physical and mental abuse that when he said he will kill me I yelled and said, "I WILL KILL MYSELF." I was so fed up with the anger that I just wanted out. I grabbed the longest knife I could find out of the knife block to kill myself but before I could commit the act he tried to tackle me again to stop me. I turned the knife from myself to him and stabbed him with it.

My mind was spinning. After I committed this act he ran from me and this was the first time he was actually scared of me which I have to admit it felt good. I wasn't the one getting hit this time or scared for my life. I had a crazy moment and chased him around the table so he could get out the house but he wouldn't leave.

Let me remind you all once again that we were both in our towels and in a situation where our heads was screwed up. He ran upstairs and I ran out the house with the knife still in my hand. I cried and cried and cried some more. I couldn't believe I was in this situation. He was bleeding profusely so he called the ambulance and they came to pick him up. By this time I was back in the house and had clothes on. They questioned him but the story he told the police was a lie to save me from getting in trouble. I think about that moment and I always asked myself, why did he lie? Was it to protect me so I wouldn't get locked up or was it because he knew I was at a boiling point from his abuse and maybe he felt like he deserved it.

As time went on I understood that this situation was the first time I really saw God working in my favor. I say that because, as you've read in the poem, sometime after that day we broke up so he put a warrant out for my arrest. He didn't say anything about me stabbing him when we stayed together but when I broke up with him he decided to call the authorities on me.

Detectives knocked on my door and asked was I familiar with a stabbing situation. I told them the truth and they took me to the precinct to question me. After my confession a police officer handcuffed me and took me to the jail to get booked. I remember the office saying, "I don't know if I want to take her in my car because I'm honestly afraid by looking at these charges." Basically the officer saw my charges and feared for his life. He started talking to me as we rode to the jail and he realized that I wasn't who the charges said I was.

We got to the jail and I had to wait to get stripped down to make sure I didn't have anything hiding in my hair or body. I was finger printed and then saw the commissioner who set my bail for 45,000 dollars. The guys in the jail started yelling out to me and one of the police officers looked at my charges and started calling me "stabber." It was like a crazy house but thankfully my mother bailed me out before I got fully processed to get suited.

My court date came and I was more than nervous but Peter didn't show up so the case got dismissed. I walked out the court room with joy and I didn't thank God then but I thank Him now because that was the first time I truly felt free from Peter and those demons. I could finally breathe again. I wasn't confined under strict law anymore and the relief on my family's face, especially my sister and mother's, was a moment I will always remember. It wasn't just me that was free but we were all free.

A Message to Peter

When you came into my life we were both broken with joy. We wore our pain well and longed for someone to fix it. We became each other's handymen. We vowed to love each other unconditionally not knowing that we were pushing each other off the deep end. We didn't know we were toxic for each other because all we knew was pain and our pain united disguised as love. I want to take this moment to tell you I'm sorry. I'm sorry for being a vehicle for Satan and I'm sorry for making you feel less than. Peter what you have to realize is that the power Satan had over us was strong and we took it out on each other. It was so powerful that I remember you were trying to go to church at one point but I was against it because I was evil. We were evil to one another and all God could do was end our situation in a way where it was a lesson for both of us. God never wants his child to be abused or hurt but oppression will produce thoughts and display actions that aren't really them. I'm also sorry for not really being me. I am not apologizing to you because I have to but I am doing so because I see the difference in flesh and spirit and now I understand the way of the enemy. The abuse I endured from you was the violence that Satan had against my love for you. He didn't want you to be loved and vice versa. Peter you have to understand that we are children of God which means that love is forbidden in Satan's eyes because love is what God unconditionally gives us. I forgive you Peter once again not because I have to but because I choose to walk in freedom. I will not be bound by the mind games that the devil had over me and I understand as I stated before that we were just the puppets and the devil was one making us dance. Be free Peter and walk in excellence and I will do the same.

I'm free

Britt

LIFE LESSONS FROM PART 2

- 🌹 Stayed longer then I should have
- 🌹 Kept my mouth shut about the abuse
- 🌹 Got into a relationship for the wrong reasons
- 🌹 Left love in his hands instead of loving myself
- 🌹 Think that I could change him

I can honestly say I stayed so long because I thought I loved him, I was trying to show him a different type of love then what he knew, and I felt emotionally attached to his situation. He needed someone in his life that could love him pass his pain as well as I so the abuse was something I tolerated in the midst of wanting to show him I cared. He is really a great person but the time I came into his life was a time where he and I needed to be alone to heal but instead we were destructive together. I can even go further and say I was trying to change him. I know I know I understand a person cannot be changed when they are stuck in their ways. It makes since now but at the time I really wanted him to love me as much as I loved him and to show it without the abuse but that didn't happen.

If you have been mentally, verbally, sexually, emotionally, or physically abused please reach out for help. There are so many women shelters, homes, organizations, churches, even strangers who will help you. Please don't stay in that situation and know that God is with you. Right now you feel like God doesn't love you because you are still in that situation but understand that once you cry out to Him He will rescue you and lead you to freedom. If you think hard enough there is someone in your life that cares enough to help you but you're so silent that they don't know. I couldn't see pass Peter and thought that no one could love me after him because I was so damaged but there is someone who will treat you better. You don't think so right now but in time you can either wait for the better or die trying to hold onto "prince charming". You might not die physically but a mental and emotional death means that he has won. It's time for you to live again.

Diary Entry (lost date)
"Omg!!!!! I just woke up and saw my father's head floating down from my bedroom door. He didn't have a body at all but just a floating head coming down from the door. I just screamed extremely loud but nobody heard me which is weird. What if I was in danger or something? I don't know if this means my father is watching over me or if the devil is trying to scare me because I have now broke up with my ex and maybe he needs to find a way to keep fear in me, who knows. I know one thing if I wasn't scared of the dark before, I am beyond scared now."

Part 3:

"New" Love

Thank you
07/19/2009-07/20/2009

I try to search for reasons to find
something wrong with you
Maybe you'll threaten, hit, or yell at me like he use to
His threat turned to your kiss
His hit turned to your soft touch
His screams turned to the words that I longed for someone to say
and actually mean
"I Love you" is what you said to me
Went from someone who uses their hands to strike me to using it
to hug me
Went from hate to love
Went from bruises to hickeys
You don't understand how you make my body quiver
My legs shiver and everything in between
I wait for you to be mean or change
I wait for you to become this person filled with rage
And wait for you to do something so I can say, "I don't trust you"
and prove that like all other dudes you're the same
But you're not
You give me joy and the world
Your time and the title of being your girl
Understanding and demanding but in a good way
I love everything about you in every single way
I finally found my true love
Someone I can call my own
Thank you for rescuing me because
I was confused and alone
Thank you

 *G*etting over the previous relationship was hard but I had my freedom back. I had a pep in my step, I was finally happy, and most of all I was single again. I was happy that I could go back to my female "player" ways and have comfort in that profession. I never knew that I could tolerate so much abuse but I had to move on. I started walking with my head up high and I didn't feel ashamed of myself. I was working so I had something to call my own and most of all my household was peaceful again. I lost my family's trust during that relationship so to elevate from that whole situation meant a lot to me. They endured a large quantity of hurt because my heart was so cold that I showed no love towards them. I only cared about Peter. They tried their best to rescue me but in return they received the most evil malicious monstrous part of me. I thank God that through it all they stuck with me because they knew that that was not my true self.

A few months later I met a guy through my best male friend at the time. We are going to name him John. John was the total opposite of Peter. I saw from the beginning that he was caring, loving, sweet, protective, and gentle. He was everything I should've had in the beginning but sometimes you have to go through a bad situation to appreciate a better one. Through John I experienced so much love and compassion that it didn't take long for me to fall in love with him. We were inseparable.

When I got locked up in the previous relationship I was actually involved with John so the transition from relationships was quick. When John found out I was in jail I didn't know if he would stay with me. I thought he would view me as someone tied to drama but he understood the situation and continued our relationship. I vividly remember him saying that that's when he knew he was in love with me because he didn't know if I was coming back. That was probably the sweetest thing any male ever spoke to me. I was either previously use to physical compliments or verbal attacks from Peter. It was refreshing to be in a situation where I didn't have to worry about any of that.

John comes from a church going family which allowed me to frequently attend church. Baptist church was different from the Catholic Church that I was use to growing up. The main difference is the music, the preaching, and the length of time the service was held. I looked pass that because I was just happy to be with someone who had a great foundation and treated me like a human being and not a toy. John and I were together for 3 ½ years and within those years I learned so much about myself. We basically grew up together. I learned how to take someone else's feelings in consideration, how to unconditionally love, and experienced what true happiness really was.

I loved this man with every fiber of my being but I must've been cursed because everything good always seemed to turn bad in my life. The turning point in our relationship was when I cheated on him. I know, I know you're thinking why would you cheat on someone who was good to you. Let me explain. At this time in my life, I was in my early 20's so I started partying a little more and going to clubs including drinking and smoking weed.

The first time I smoked was with my friends at the time and being around professionals I didn't really know my limit. I just wanted to keep up. We smoked a lot that night. I'd never been high before so now my eyes and mind opened up to a whole new world that I was not ready to encounter. I didn't want John to know I was smoking that night but he kept calling me for some reason to see where I was. It was like he knew I was doing something wrong. I tried to lie and say I caught contact but he did not believe that. Just to clarify, catching contact is when a person is in an intimate space with someone who is smoking marijuana and feels high from the smoke. The person who caught contact did not smoke but it feels like they did.

John was so mad at me for a couple reasons: 1. I made him stop smoking because it reminded me of my father, 2. I lied to him about it. I lied to him because I made him stop smoking and I didn't want to look like a hypocrite. I never smoked in my life before this and every time a male crossed my path they smoked including my father and my ex. I guess the night I decided to try it was because I was curious and I can honestly say I was being a follower. This brings me to the night I cheated. I was around a couple of people and we had drinks, smoked weed, and ate weed brownies. Everyone was watching television and eventually it got late. I was sitting beside one of the guys there, he decided to pull out his penis, and I decided to react with my hand. It went on for literally a couple seconds because I felt bad and I know that even though it was a small situation I still cheated. I told John about it and he was so mad. It took a lot of arguments and healing but he ended up forgiving me.

Weed Demon

I felt a lustful feeling in my Ora
Opening up to each stroke from him
I never knew this would feel this good
It was like my insides wanted more and I never got sore, it was
amazing
I found the cure to the deepness I was longing for
But I wanted more
More sex meant more drugs and more drugs meant less of God's
love

I wanted the connection but in my mind
I wasn't done knocking at the devils door
There was one time I smoked and God had enough of it
So I threw up over and over and over and over again
I felt paralyzed like my insides were collapsing in
I'm thinking in my mind God I have sinned AGAIN
But I'm immune to this feeling
And didn't want anything to stop me
until The Lord showed himself in the darkness of my room
tapping me
I didn't want to wake up so I groaned as my defense
God tapped harder and harder on my shoulder
until I woke up in his presence
I didn't see him but I could see him
I instantly knew to wake up and praise him
Up for two hours praying everything that could come to my mind
to say to him
Like God please forgive me for my sins,
I'll never smoke weed again
Now 3 o'clock in the morning has been my prayer time
with the Lord ever since
Over the course of 8 months I battled with that demon
Because it wasn't just weed but fornication
was the true demon
But God showed me the book of Job and
that's where my life is leading
Call me holy if you want but I gave the devil
too much time and freedom
In my life he's locked in a box and it's no keys to open it
I don't care if he suffers
He's taking too many of my brothers, it's no way I will open it
You wait until the rapture comes then you'll get released
where your soul is
And I'll be floating to my father to the kingdom
where my home is
10 months ago was my last time
It's no way I could write poetry, sing,
and still smoke in my spare time

God will change your whole mindset about
what life really is
and the actual purpose of your being
Because the devil attacks your thoughts
and if you let him it's no way he's fleeing
Don't let being unsure keep you from God
because your answers will get answered
when you take the steps toward the kingdom
So if these words relate to you
then this is confirmation that the battle in your head is
between God and god and I call him the weed demon

One day John and I decided to smoke together for the first time and boy was that an experience. The level of lust and fornication that happened that night elevated my feelings for him from love to the highest level of lust I never knew was there. This is what I meant by my eyes and mind opening up to a whole new world I wasn't ready for. My body felt like a whole new person and the level of freak that came out of my body was jaw dropping. One can say we found a new dangerous hobby together because a couple that smokes together is now spiritually tied in more toxic levels then one can know.

Literally, both of you will walk and talk alike without even trying. One will start to get angry when the other has done something without him/her when they usually do it together. In addition, the level of jealousy goes through the roof. It's almost as if that person cannot breathe without the other knowing because of the insanity of feeling left out. After that couple breaks up the bond won't break because the intimacy won't be the same with someone else unless they are high.

What you need to understand is when the penis enters the vagina, whatever spirits that person is carrying is now in you. It got to a point where I didn't want to have sex unless we smoked because that was the feeling I expected. There are no limits when you mix marijuana and sex because your mind, body, and soul are not you anymore.

A person can imagine whatever they want and portray those actions while having sex and the other will see that as attractive and a turn on because they find it freaky. What actually is happening is they are looking at a spirit act. That spirit is a gruesome demon but since I was in a relationship and I loved John, I saw it as a bonding experience we shared and the way we showed love to each other. Weed was a part of our relationship for a while. It was such of an expectancy that I would get upset if John smoked without me as I just stated. It got to a point where the weed took over and the relationship was just for title, it was no longer the focus. After 3 ½ years there was no growth and being together was a waste of time especially when there was something being birthed inside of me. I know some of you are thinking a baby, but no, I mean my walk with Christ was manifesting inside of me but I had to separate from John to deliver it.

It took a long while for me to stop dealing with John because the process of getting over a long term soul tied relationship can take time. We talked about having a child and what our future would be like so to erase all of those good and bad memories out of my mind took some time. After we broke up we still dealt with each other sexually including smoking and drinking as well. We would rent continuous motel rooms and spend the night together.

It was like the spirit didn't want to let me go. Just like the poem, "Weed Demon" said, I remember on one of our motel excursions that I couldn't stop throwing up after we smoked. It was almost as if God was pushing the weed out of me because my insides felt like every bone was breaking. Every time I threw up my stomach would tighten up, which is normal, but it was like I stopped breathing after each time. I had to gasp for air a couple of times because it felt like I was dying and I know it sounded like it. I remember hearing voices laughing at me in my head as I was in that bathroom. What's funny is how cunning it is because when John and I communicated he would bring up past memories about our relationship knowing that I would ponder them.

Once my mind was where he wanted it he knew he could get me to comply. That's how the devil works. He will skillfully get you to a sinful place where you think it is ok because it's a familiar situation, he'll display his true intentions, and then act as if nothing happened after he gets what he wants. One might say, "Nobody made you do it. You came here on your own." Yes you did but because you thought one thing and had no clue about the other until you got there.

Queen, you might've gotten tricked once but don't let the devil fool you again with the same agenda. I was comfortable in my sin so I kept going back for physical temporary comfort but in the end I was just hurting myself. I had no real satisfaction. I don't personally blame John for any of our sexual encounters because through him I have full knowledge of the how the devil works. God works in so many ways and I'm here to inform you so you won't have to experience this yourself.

Or do you not know that your body is the temple of the Holy Spirit who is in you are not your own? For you were bought at a price: therefore glorify God in your body (1 Corinthians 6:19,20)

This dream was really distinct and detailed. It started with another scene but that isn't the importance of why I'm mentioning it. The second scene began with a group of females including myself who were run a ways. We lived in a motel room packed together and nowhere to go. For some reason I had a little brother with me but it was weird because in real life I don't have a brother.

All of a sudden he left the room so a couple of girls and I ran to go look for him. I found him outside in the dark in an alley way crying on the ground and sitting Indian style. I ran to hug him and brought him back to the room because it wasn't safe outside alone. As we were walking to the room a group of gay people ran out of there hiding place and tried to attack us. They were also run a ways and needed somewhere to stay so they tried to take our room. Every girl who lived with me started fighting them off and they eventually left. This happened three times with three different groups of people trying to come and take our room. I can't remember who the second group of people was but we did defeat them. My brother was so scared. He hid under the table in the room until the second batch left.

I found him once again and gave him a huge hug to comfort him. Once I realized we weren't going to sleep that night and maybe more people would try to come I hid him in the closet with my earphones to make sure he couldn't hear anything. The third group barged in the room like they owned the place and started to take over the room. They were a bunch of crips and bloods both male and female. All of a sudden music started playing and everyone began to dance with each other.

It was as if there was a lustful trance that took over. None of the girls started to fight them or realized that this group is here for the same reason the other groups were. I even started to dance for a couple seconds but then I snapped out of it and realized what was going on. I tapped each girl and said, "HELLO HELLO is anybody going to fight with me or IGNORE ME AND KEEP DANCING." They paid me no attention and that's when I realized I was on my own. A couple of the gang members saw me yelling and realized their trance didn't work on me. They started walking towards me and I started walking towards the closet where my brother was. They tried to get to him but I wouldn't let them so it was me against about ten of them. One by one each person charged towards me.

Next thing I know is I saw each one flying across the room because I had that much power in me to take them all. One girl who was a crip said ,"Man watch out I can take her." So we started to fight and I beat her so bad that she started to spin in circles so my punches wouldn't land. While all this is going on in the corner the lustful trance is still happening and none of the girls came to fight with me. At that moment I stopped, closed my eyes, and saw the beautiful blue sky and fluffy white clouds. I proceeded to pray and said, "God I can't do this anymore." Then I woke up

This dream made no since in the beginning because as I said I don't have a brother. But as I began to seek God it was confirmed that the little brother was John and he was telling me that I don't have to feel obligated to him. Since we had so much history I was so attached to him that for a while he was the person I went to for everything even after the breakup. I wanted to love him so much that I stayed longer then I should have. When we get in the way of God we fight other people's battle when it isn't meant for us. It may be hard but stay obedient and do what God asks of you.

After all of the partying, backsliding, and constant sinning with John God gave me this dream telling me that I was overstaying my welcome. I have this tendency of holding onto people in my life which is why it took so long for me to leave the abusive relationship. I was scared for a male to leave me because it would always remind me of my father so I held on. John was not only someone I loved but we were in the longest relationship I'd been in so I didn't know how to let go but I had to. When the Lord tells you it's time to go, then it's time to go. I thank God for giving me this dream and confirming in my present life that all I have to do is wait on Him and he will send me the person who is right for me.

Treasure Chest
03/10/2014-03/20/2014

(Blessings will come once you give your life to him)
She is a lonely girl filled with anger hoping maybe one day her
prince will someday give her a kiss under the mistletoe
Every night she weeps about what she doesn't have and has to be
the referee of the fights between her mom and dad
Nothing but yelling and screaming around her, covering her ears
every night before she goes to sleep
Hoping that someday she will be taken away from the constant
pain and misery
It's nobody she trusts cuz the house she lives in doesn't look like
much
So she started to confide in her friends until one of them decide
she looked good enough to touch
6 years old never knew what lust was until she decided to bring
her into that cross fire
The devil said you asked for this
You said you wanted out and can't take any more pain and
misery
Well let's see what happens when I force you to become the
woman I want you to be
Years go by and the lust gets bigger
She finds out the party life is her scene cuz no one begs to differ
A good girl on the inside a fake bad girl on the out
Attracts bad boys on the inside and real bad boys on the out
See the first hit shocked her
The second hit was ok
By the third she was numb and became tolerant to pain
(Blessings will come once you give your life to him)
But one day her mind shifts and realize she wants to live
Until now living in the dark was ok cuz back then life wasn't in
the house where she lived
See but God always has a plan in store for you

Cuz when you don't see him he sees you
That feeling she felt didn't come out the blue
That was the tugging between God and Satin in a spiritual battle
So ladies love the skin you're in and forget about your mistakes
you made in your past
Once you become obedient God will rescue you from that bozo
and send you your Boaz
Don't give into the devils lies
he tried to trick Eve into thinking by eating the fruit her and
Gods power would be equal
But see being a born again believer only makes Satin mad cuz he
knows that sin doesn't have power over dead people.
Women stop walking with your head down
Jesus will never turn his back on you, but to seek him you gotta
pray up that's the only way blessings will come down
They say you can't turn a hoe into a housewife
Well I beg to differ
Cuz the little girl in the beginning of the story was me
and God gave this ex hoe a mission so a housewife is not in my
destiny
Giving my life to Christ was the only thing that saved her
See once you know his glory, you realize it's not about your body
but the heart inside of your chest is the treasure

A Message to John

It took me a very long time to get over you. I must say soul ties are a beast. You not only had my body but you had my mind, spirit, and heart. It wasn't just physical or emotional with you but it was spiritual as well. Only you and I know how deep the rabbit hole goes between us and honestly for a long time I wanted that hole to stay deep. I was with you when God called me to walk with Christ and the specific instruction from Him was to separate from you but I didn't. I loved you too much and somewhere in my head I knew that I could make it work but I was wrong. I asked God why am I so tied to you and why after the back and forth torment do I continue to put myself through conviction even after we broke up. He told me that it's deeper then you and to not look at you as the reason why I sin. Just like Peter and I, you were just the vehicle. I couldn't be blinded by the fact that you treated me better then Peter because that's why I stayed. He wanted me to see the operation behind the scenes.

I carried the same spirits from my childhood and from Peter in the relationship with you but there was something else I missed. I understood a certain level of evil because I lived it and I operated with it but I didn't know your type. I was use to open anger and the display of exposed cruelty but yours were secretive and witty.

Your demons were wiser then me and you knew how to play the game. You could serenade my mind with words and speak to me in a way where you knew I would accept it. Your spirits could talk their way out of anything and everything because their cunning ways are secret to the extreme. They are very dangerous but quite frankly you know that already. I never knew them until I met you but until God elevated me to a level where I could pray against them then going back to you would've been my only choice. I wasn't strong enough to leave. I thank God for showing me what that looks like because I now know a different level of Satan's games. God has a plan for everything and opening my eyes to see the truth disconnects me from ill feelings towards you. I have found my peace in the Lord and I thank God that He reassures me every day that the only communication we need is prayer. Prayer is powerful because a person can get delivered with it and let me tell you John that I am delivered from it all.

I'm free

Britt

- Wait until I fully healed before getting into another relationship
- Listened to God instead of rekindling emotions that should have stayed closed
- Loved and respected myself more

Ladies these sexual feelings will try their best to keep you shackled even if it means making decisions that is displeasing to God. As I stated God was calling me so it was no way these feelings would let me go that easily but I thank God for rescuing me from that situation. It took a long long long time to leave but I finally made the decision to remove all communication and to finally live for Christ. Just like Peter, John is a great person. He was literally the prince charming I was longing for but I was still broken. I was now two relationships in and was still empty. As I stated God was calling me to walk with Christ toward the end of our relationship and He did that because He wanted to show me that He could restore any emptiness I had. I looked for my relationships to do it but nothing worked. I decided to try God because as I said nothing else worked and boy am I glad I made that decision.

Part 4

God Found Me

Psalm 139:14
I praise thee that I am fearfully and
wonderfully made
Marvelous are thy works and my soul
knoweth right well

66

I know everything you have done, and you are not cold or hot. I wish you were either one or the other. But since you are lukewarm and neither cold nor hot, I will spit you out of my mouth. You claim to be rich and successful and to have everything you need. But you don't know how badly off you are. You are pitiful, poor, blind, and naked. Buy your gold from me. It has been refined in a fire, and it will make you rich. Buy white clothes from me. Wear them and you can cover up your shameful nakedness. Buy medicine for your eyes, so that you will be able to see. (Revelation 3:15-18 CEVUK00)

(lost date) 2013
Just had a dream and I saw a white figure the size of a young boy but I couldn't see his face. The figure moved really slow and graceful and it said, "Come, Come". It was a pitch black background and I wasn't sure what the figure was or why it said come but it was a dream that stuck out in my head for so long.

I had that dream three years ago and that was the

beginning of God calling me to walk with Jesus. Sometime after John and I broke up, I was invited to a church, by a woman who I call my spiritual mother until this day, and really liked it. She was that nurturing mother figure that didn't accept back talk or attitude and that's what I needed.

Everyone was friendly and I started to meet Christ like people who were very different from the folks I hung around. They welcomed me with open arms and at that moment God had my attention. In the beginning I didn't join the church but I only went to the bible studies because I wanted to get a feel for it first. Bible study was awesome because that is where I understood why I had the dream above. We were in the book of Matthew and this is what it said:

Matthew 14:22-33:
Immediately Jesus made His disciples get into the boat and go before Him to the other side, while He sent the multitudes away. And when He had sent the multitudes away, He went up on the mountain by Himself to pray. Now when evening came, He was alone there. But the boat was now in the middle of the sea, tossed by the waves, for the wind was contrary. Now in the fourth watch of the night Jesus went to them, walking on the sea. And when the disciples saw Him walking on the sea, they were troubled, saying, "It is a ghost!" And they cried out for fear. But immediately Jesus spoke to them, saying, "Be of good cheer! It is I; do not be afraid." And Peter answered Him and said, "Lord, if it is You, command me to come to You on the water." So He said, "Come." And when Peter had come down out of the boat, he walked on the water to go to Jesus. But when he saw that the wind was boisterous, he was afraid: and beginning to sink he cried out, saying, "Lord save me!" And immediately Jesus stretched out his hand and caught him, and said to him, "O you of little faith, why did you doubt?" And when they got into the boat,

the wind ceased. Then those who were in the boat came and worshipped Him saying, "Truly You are the Son of God."

Jesus told Peter to come to Him and to not be afraid, which is the same thing God asked of me in my dream. That word "come" meant that God was calling me and this scripture made it so clear. Peter walked on water but sank because he was afraid and I realized I had to make a decision of will I walk towards Jesus and take steps to leave my old ways or sink with Satan. I decided to walk with Christ and not long after I joined the church.

I didn't know what was really happening to me because I didn't know how God worked or even who He was so when He showed up one night in my room I was terrified. It was like an awakening. I was sleep and all of a sudden I felt tapping on my shoulder about 3 o'clock in the morning. I woke up so terrified that I immediately started praying. I didn't know much about prayer at the time but the little bit I did know is what I used. I stayed up for about two hours and the intimate prayer time I had with God was so comforting and peaceful that I knew for sure that God is real and He is everything I was missing in my life.

Sometimes, when a person is called to walk with Christ or makes that life changing decision on their own, it can be very scary because it's new and the total opposite of what's expected. In the beginning I was the most stubborn, imperfect, but happy Christian there is because I didn't know how to act. I was excited about making a life changing decision but still operating in my own mindset and didn't let God fully work in my life.

As you read prior, I was hurt from the abandonment of my father and I had so many issues that I couldn't bear to let God run my whole entire life without having just a little bit of control. I was still in the relationship with John when God called me and I didn't want to stop what we had going on.

Honestly, I didn't know how to fully believe in something or a "spirit" that was not there or that I couldn't see so living the carnal life was what I went back to. Even though I had the encounter with God I didn't have a relationship with Him to appreciate what happened. What's ironic is John was raised in the church so when God called me I just knew we would have this Christian relationship but I was wrong. We actually started sinning more as you read in Part 3 and once the devil realized I actually wanted to accept Christ he made sure the soul tie I had with John did not let loose.

This caused so much confusion for me because, in my mind, saying yes to God meant my troubles were over. It meant I was going to have a perfect Christian life and all of my issues would be washed away. Boy was I fooled. Saying yes to God bought more demons my way because Satan was now angry that I chose to live for the light and not the darkness he knew of me. I joined a church, went to bible study faithfully, and never missed a Sunday service. I felt like I was going above and beyond and doing all of the right things that I was supposed to do. Keep in mind when you are a babe in Christ, you will be a follower for some years until you get to know God for yourself.

A babe is someone who is immature spiritually and in the beginning stages of knowing who Christ is. That is who I was and who you will be when you accept Christ as your Lord and Savior until time allows you to really know him. I had to learn through much heart ache, wrong decisions, and understanding that Jesus is God who formed himself to be a man to come to earth to die for our sins. Maybe some of you are asking, "Why would God do this just to die?"

Understand that God is Spirit who loves us dearly and in order for our sins to be saved this is what he had to do because what he tried before didn't work. Thousands of years before Jesus was formed, God saw that the world was violently corrupted by man. In the Book of Genesis God instructed Noah to build an ark because the world that He created was in turmoil.

Genesis 6:11-13 and 7:4 states: The earth also was corrupt before God, and the earth was filled with violence. So God looked upon the earth, and indeed it was corrupt; for the flesh has corrupted their way on the earth. And God said to Noah, "The end of all flesh has come before Me, for the earth is filled with violence through them: and behold, I will destroy them with the earth. "For after seven more days I will cause it to rain on the earth forty days and forty nights, and I will destroy from the face of the earth all living things that I have made."

When God created the world he didn't create the people to be as cruel and violent as they became. God was angry with them so he bought on a great flood to destroy all things living except for Noah, his family, and the animals the Lord told Noah to take with him. Noah was the only one of that generation who was faithful to the Lord and believed in Him so Noah is who God used to start over.

This brings us to why God formed into flesh and became Jesus. God understood that, because of Satan, this world and the people in it will continue to sin. If God wanted to, He could've kept bringing on floods and continuously destroying people to start over but he didn't because His plan is not to destroy us but to save us. The only way we could be saved was if someone who is sinless dies for our sins.

Would you want to die for my sins? Would you die for the sins of people you don't know? I'm pretty sure your answer would probably be no because you don't know me but God knows and loves everybody because He created us. Everything you see and everyone you know is His creation. He loved us enough to become flesh and suffer on our behalf because He knew that sin will not go away. Honestly, I wouldn't know if I would have the courage to endure what Jesus did but I can say that I am so grateful because without crucifixion I wouldn't be

71

able to repent for my wrongdoing which in the end will save me from hell.

My main reason for walking with Christ was because I didn't want to go to hell but in time I've learned that Christianity is much more than staying out of hell and looking and acting like a "Christian". It's about understanding who God designed you to be and walking in that. Sometimes many of us won't find our individual path until we actually make the decision to give our lives to Christ because if our family isn't following Him then we will never know who we are really supposed to be.

As I sat in church and listened to every sermon my mind started to understand God's word but I never connected with it because growing up Catholic caused my mind to have a disconnect. Catholics believe that God and Jesus are two different people but the word clearly states that it's all God.

1 John 5:7- For there are three that bear witness in heaven: the Father, the Word, and the Holy Spirit; and these three are one.

Once I started to read the Word for myself, overtime my wounds started to heal and my emptiness started to get filled just like God promised. Please don't think that it will happen overnight because it won't but accepting Christ let's God know that you are serious about deliverance and it tells him that you want to be free. Honestly, I was the same person after I accepted Christ as I was before but the difference was that I decided to let God fix those places and I got out of the way. *Psalm 23:3 says, "He restores my soul".*

One by one as this was actually happening, I started to connect with the Bible more because I treated it as God speaking to me and not just words on a page. I saw the joy creeping in and I hadn't felt joy since before I was molested. I was happy but I didn't have joy. The difference is this: Happiness has a limit and it can only come from man but joy comes from God and it's a feeling that no one can give you but Him. This is why I continue to seek Him and believe in His way because to no longer be angry at all of the hurt I endured is nothing but a miracle. The only way we can know about God and discerning his voice is by reading about Him and believing what we read.

Discerning or discernment means that God is applying spiritual guidance to a person so they will be informed on things they spiritually don't know. In the Old Testament we see the Lord speak and in the New Testament we see Jesus speak. You can't know God's voice without reading the way He speaks because when He guides you you'll know that it's Him.

On the other hand, there are a lot of people that mimic Christianity but being a Christian has nothing to do with looks but everything to do with your actions and the purity of your heart. When God found me I was so broken and I trusted no one but if God can call a filthy sex crazed pornographic watching weed smoking person like me then he can do the same for you.

You can be a prostitute, a liar, a deceiver, homosexual, a sex addict, a binge addict, suicidal, homicidal, a pimp, a drug addict, and anything else that is not pleasing in his sight and God will wash you from those sins and free you. I just wanted to be free and once I repented for my sins he did that for me.

Luke 15:4-7 says: "What man of you, having a hundred sheep, if he loses one of them, does not leave the ninety-nine in the wilderness, and go after the one which is lost until he finds it? "And when he comes home, he calls together his friends and neighbors, saying to them, `Rejoice with me, for I have found my sheep which was lost!` " I say to you that likewise there will be more joy in heaven over one sinner who repents then over ninety-nine just persons who need no repentance.

When we repent for our sins angels rejoice in heaven because that is one less person the devil has a hold of. So I ask, "Who do you live for?" Do you live for the devil who wants to keep you in an open jail cell that looks lavish right now but in the end will send you to hell? I loved having sex, smoking, drinking, and getting attention from boys but that did nothing for me.

I kept going back to it but the satisfaction was temporary. Satan made everything look great because I felt beautiful from those compliments but I was still dying inside. I had layers of stuff to get out of me but the devil did nothing but pile on the hurt. Or, do you live for Christ who died for your sins and will internally heal you so you'll feel beautiful on your own. God found me in my darkness and He will find you to. The satisfaction the Lord gives me is beyond a quick fix. It is eternal because as I stated before He permanently restored those empty spots and that is something that cannot be broken again. So I ask again," Who do you live for"?

Who do you live for?
08/12/2013

Melody:
When day comes and night falls
For the rest of our lives we'll miss ya'll
And even though life must go on, we still mourn
While wishing ya'll were home

The truth is, everybody's not going to make it in
Lord I pray for those who don't know you
in the pardon of their sins
In the beginning the Word was God
So if the Word is with God and you have the Word
and God in your Spirit,
then that's how you make it in
Not going to church to fill up a seat then leave and smoke and drink for
a week
See we are the salt of the earth
Too many people try to be sugar and make everything sweet
Don't forget people hated Jesus
We're not here to make friends to set up meet and greets
We're here to spread God's Word and the bible says if no one is
receiving peace
Then take that peace back and wipe the dust off your feet
God sees who is down for him
He takes the time to show his children that he's down for them
Name one person who would take a beating for those who know they
will sin again
And still say I love and forgive you because you're my sin again
So make a decision
Are you a wheat or a tare
Are you a child of God or a child of wicked one
I can't fathom thinking I'm ok then judgment day I get kicked from my
birth place
Because I didn't honor the Lord who resides in my birthplace
I mean what more do I have to say
Hell is real and the devil doesn't care anything about God's grace

75

See beauty is in the eye of the one who holds our destiny
Forget heaven I love God so much I want to be where ever he will be
He's the same God that helped the blind man see
The same God that turned the woman away from sin and adultery
He's the same God that helped 5,000 men eat and if you're not
convinced he's all powerful yet, he's the same God that tells the devil
where to flee
See before I held back about expressing my love for Christ
because of how I was judged especially by the wicked people
But I stand tall in my Spirit
I'll be that marvelous light, I mean Jesus had to
If you not called out of darkness then it's not your time yet
But keep pushing forward because the Lord is waiting for you to
detach from the devil's antics
See we don't have to wear our cross, to wear our cross
Because when times get hard were obligated to lean on God
We have to separate from the flesh it's our only way home
So when the Lord releases his Spirit from this world
We will sing this song

Melody:
When night falls and day comes
His spirit rise with all of the Christians
And even though life might seem rough
It's never tough because we're on our way home

Spiritual Battle

I had to ask this question myself a lot in this walk because, as my internal wounds were healing and I became more engulfed in God's word, I was still battling with those demons. Who do I live for? Sometimes my actions would say I live for Satan but my heart would say I live for Christ. This is called a spiritual battle. I don't ever want you to think that making a decision to walk with Christ means your problems will go away instantly because they won't.

When you see Christians who look perfect it's because they either don't talk about their sins, act like their sins don't exist, or has been healed and are walking in deliverance and freedom. At this stage in my life I am open about my past but I also hid my sins because I was ashamed. I didn't want people to know my deepest darkest secrets even though it's always someone who could relate.

I let sex run my life. I would put myself in border line prostitute situations and was actually proud of it because I "thought" I was in control. Let's make one thing clear, I am not a prostitute, but I basically knew if a male texted or called my phone to go out I knew the aftermath would be sex. It's an exchange deal between two people that's unspoken but it's expected to happen because of soul ties. It's like you speak the same language without speaking. These demons are so dangerous to operate with because as you're moving day to day you really think you're thinking normally but you're not. Your body is moving and your mind is thinking but it's not you.

As a Christian I was still in church praising the Lord but the devil makes things looks like God when it's not. I was operating in an oppressed state when I first joined the church but moving functionally as a normal person does. In order to understand the difference between whom you really are and who the devil tries to manipulate you to be is knowledge. If you know something is wrong don't justify your actions just to make it seem ok. IT'S A SIN, DON'T DO IT!!!! Knowledge is power and I can display all of my sins to you right now because I've been used up so much that it's no way I can bear to make the same mistakes over and over again. It has to be a point in your life where you say enough is enough. If you want the same knowledge, read your word and God will tell you everything you need to know.

Pornography

Speaking of displaying my sins, let's elaborate on pornography. It is sex displayed on screen that leaves continuous images in your head so it's prone to come out and act. It's sort of like a movie. A person who battles with lust and fornication is guaranteed to battle with pornography because it all comes together. Queens if you have the reputation of being called loose or a hoe, which are all horrible words, understand why you act this way.

When I would have sex those images from a video would pop in my head. This would trick a person to think I'm enjoying them but I'm really thinking about the pornography. As I got older I started to view different types of videos that eventually became normal to watch. For example, I would watch cartoons, anime characters, same sex females, transgender females, and even weird looking monster type characters that would have sex with normal looking anime females.

If you battle with this and especially if you watch the same types of videos I watched understand how this works. As you read earlier, I'd been watching pornography and masturbating since I was six years old, so I've seen it elevate from low grade videos to high definition movies. The story line looks so real life that you start to make it your own life or trick your mind to think you're just watching a regular movie. The next morning you will start to remember those sexual voices, sounds, and images that you'll hear it in your mind randomly in your day to day. Those thoughts will put you in a trance or you'll day dream about it. Then, when your mind comes back into focus you'll look around in paranoia to make sure no one sees your facial expression from your trance or hears your thoughts when in actuality it's all in your mind.

Furthermore, the creators of the cartoon pornography will use real shows and make sex scenes from them. So, basically if you watch that cartoon in real life you are going to think of that pornographic video even though it is an innocent show. Your mind will have no peace. Do you see how this works? Pornography is demonic!! It even got to a point where I got to know the names of certain males and specifically searched for a video that I knew I could masturbate to with them in it. It got pretty sick and everything I saw on those videos was things I would do in person.

The intensity of lust that would happen in person was unbelievable to me once I came out of my trance because I was Brittany again. It's like an outer body experience and the devil plays with the mind so much that you will start to justify your actions to make it seem like somehow they're right. When you battle with lustful spirits the highlight of these sexual acts is the preparation in the mind prior.

Once that act happens it is not all what your mind said it was supposed to be. These are mind games the devil plays. He wants you to think that the images in your head and the intensity of your flesh is what your body will feel when you have sex but when you actually do it and it's over you're left disappointed because it's not what you expected. What happens is we keep going back to it because you start to go on a mission to get that feeling but the satisfaction is never there.

What I ended up doing as I stated before is smoking weed and using sex toys like vibrators and dildos. Spencer's was my favorite store. Anytime I knew I wanted to have sex I would use these because my body was able to take the deepness and pain that it couldn't when I was sober. My body has endured so much harm and I can admit that it wasn't entirely the devil's fault. Every bad decision we make is introduced by the devil because it's his agenda to kill, steal, and destroy, but it's our job to be on our "A" game at all times to resist him. Words cannot explain how embarrassed I felt when I fully understood my actions and how it made God feel. Romans 8:16-17 says, "The Spirit Himself bears witness with our spirit that we are children of God, and if children, then heirs-heirs of God and joint heirs with Christ, if indeed we suffer with Him, that we may also be glorified together."

Once I read this scripture I understood that I am a joint heir with Christ who died on the cross for me. So if I am a joint heir that means we are connected spiritually and if I'm having sex multiple times then Jesus is with me while I am doing this. I don't want to be the one who makes Jesus suffer all over again when he already died on the cross for me. You shouldn't want this either. Furthermore, I despise the devil so I definitely don't want him to be boastful to God about me for failing once again. Ever since that day I was done with those spirits.

The battle between flesh and spirit is so crucial when the mind only knows the way of Satan. It's like a lion attacking its prey for food and not letting up until that prey is captured. This is what Satan does because he will do anything to keep your soul for himself.

When I stated earlier that you cannot stop praying and reading your word, I meant that. This is the only way Satan will leave you alone. I'm not trying to scare anyone because understand that God is way bigger than the devil but we cannot defeat him by ourselves. We need God. We need Jesus. We need the Holy Spirit. We need all three and after knowing God how I do now I understand why He found me and that's because at the moment of destruction that's when I needed Him the most.

I had a dream that I was in jail. As the guards walked me to my cell I wasn't able to see the prisoners in their cells because everything was covered. I arrived at my cell and as I entered in it was so big as if it was a community room not a jail cell. The guards locked me in and all of sudden two guys came out of nowhere and tried to rape me. They kept chasing me all over the jail cell trying to get me but I kept fighting them off. These men were so much bigger and stronger than me but my strength was more powerful. More men kept coming towards me to try to get me but couldn't. As I defeated each man I threw them over the rail that was in the room but instead of them falling they actually fell into a black hole as if the other side of the rail was the portal to hell.

"This dream means that those demons that are following me are no longer in my life. They are gone and are defeated in the name of Jesus. Thank you Lord"

Part 5:

Celibacy

Psalm 139:14
I praise thee that I am fearfully and
wonderfully made
Marvelous are thy works and my soul
knoweth right well

Celibacy

Lord I finally see
I have to revisit the beginning
To the story of Adam and Eve
Before they ate from the tree

Only after was it embarrassing
To be naked before thee
Sin covered the purity
You once called free

You created them perfect
Without a covering
So Lord I ask
Take the covering from me

I give you my temple
I give you my spirit
I give you my scent
I accept this covenant

With this purity ring
I wed thee
With this purity ring
I gain celibacy

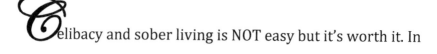

elibacy and sober living is NOT easy but it's worth it. In the beginning the process is the hardest because it's like you're in detox from sex. It sounds funny but you seriously have to fight every day to pray away those thoughts and to not let them linger. It's so easy to want to go look at pornography or call that person you know will come to pleasure you for the moment. Trust me I know a couple numbers I can call but it's not worth it. There will be times where out the blue you will get a sexual thought, pornographic image, or someone you don't know might even make a statement that reminds you of someone you've had sex with. Please I repeat please don't go back and stay strong through it because this the devils way of throwing you off. As I've stated those demons are dangerous and can easily take over because they won't leave you alone. Ignore them and they will flee. Most importantly you're not only putting your spirit in jeopardy but theirs as well. Once you keep pressing day by day it'll get easier to not act because your body has now withdrawn. It's like a drug. When you realize how easy it is you'll be so proud of yourself and will want to spread the word to people who need it. In the poem above explains how Adam and Eve were tempted by the devil:

Genesis 3:1-7 states: Now the serpent was more cunning than any beast of the field which the Lord God had made. And he said to the woman, "Has God indeed said, 'You shall not eat of every tree of the garden'?" And the woman said to the serpent, "We may eat the fruit of the trees of the garden; "but of the fruit of the tree which is in the midst of the garden, God has said, 'You shall not eat it, nor shall you touch it, lest you die.'" Then the serpent said to the woman, "You will not surely die. "For God knows that in the day you eat of it your eyes will be opened and you will be like God, knowing good and evil." So when the woman saw that the tree was good for food, that it was pleasant to the eyes, and a tree desirable to make one wise, she took of its fruit and ate. She also gave to her husband with her, and he ate. Then the eyes of both of them were opened, and they knew that they were naked; and they sewed fig trees together and made themselves coverings.

I have read this passage many times but God opened my eyes and showed me something so profound that I continuously overlooked. I always knew that Adam and Eve were always naked but I never realized they didn't know they were naked until after they sinned. As you see above they started to cover themselves after they ate from the tree and this is what we do when we sin. We try to hide from God but it's impossible to do that because God is everywhere and he is all knowing. I put this in my poem because celibacy is a spiritual purity that is made with God to be abstinent until marriage and the purity before Adam and Eve sinned is the purity I strive for. I don't want to have to cover up before God because of self-shame.

I want to be spiritually naked before God and be proud of a clean temple. Ladies, this doesn't mean you have to be a virgin to do this. You can have 10 kids with 5 different fathers or even sexually active very heavily like me, it doesn't matter. If you're not married and you decide tomorrow that you want to give your body to God, He will accept you just like He will a virgin. At my job a young lady wanted to purchase a purity ring but instead of getting the purity ring she got another one. I asked her why and she stated she has three children out of wedlock so she isn't pure. This is false. When people feel this way it is because someone told her this and I had to let her know that God accepts everybody.

You should never feel like you are unworthy of anything God has waiting for us just because it took longer to receive it. God doesn't want us to be perfect but just to make the right decisions with our bodies. Remember that whatever sin we do is a sin Jesus is enduring with us because we are a joint heir with Him.

I will always remember the date I brought my ring because it was the beginning of my true covenant with God. Two and a half years before I gave my life to Christ I had to go through hurdles to really give everything to the Lord. I had to develop the kind of faith Abraham had when God told him to sacrifice his son in order to fully understand the huge decision I made.

Genesis 22:1-19 states: Now it came to pass after these things that God tested Abraham, and said to him, "Abraham!" And he said, "Here I am." Then He said, "Take now your son, your only son Isaac, whom you love, and go to the land of Moriah, and offer him there as a burnt offering on one of the mountains of which I shall tell you." So Abraham rose early in the morning and saddled his donkey, and took two of his young men with him, and Isaac his son; and he split the wood for the burnt offering, and arose and went to the place of which God had told him. Then on the third day Abraham lifted his eyes and saw the place afar off. And Abraham said to his young men, "stay here with the donkey; the lad and I will go yonder and worship, and we will come back to you." So Abraham took the wood of the burnt offering and laid it on Isaac his son; and he took the fire in his hand, and a knife, and the two of them went together. 7 But Isaac spoke to Abraham his father and said, "My father!" And he said, "Here I am, my son." Then he said, "Look, the fire and the wood, but where is the lamb for a burnt offering?" And Abraham said, "My son, God will provide for Himself the lamb for a burnt offering." So both of them went together. Then they came to the place of which God had told him. And Abraham built an altar there and placed the wood in order; and he bound Isaac his son and laid him on the altar, upon the wood. And Abraham stretched out his hand and took the knife to slay his son. But the Angel of the LORD called to him from heaven and said, "Abraham, Abraham!" So he said, "Here I am." And He said, "Do not lay your hand on the lad, or do anything to him; for now I know that you fear God, since you have not withheld your son, your only son, from Me." Then Abraham lifted his eyes and looked, and there behind him was a ram caught in a thicket by its horns. So Abraham went and took the ram, and offered it up for a burnt offering instead of his son. And Abraham called the name of the place, The-LORD-Will-Provide; as it is said to this day, "In the Mount of the LORD it shall be provided." Then the Angel of the LORD called to Abraham a second time out of heaven, and said: "By Myself I have sworn, says the LORD, because you have done this thing, and have not withheld your son, your only son blessing I will bless you, and multiplying I will multiply your descendants as the stars of the heaven and as the sand which is on the seashore; and your descendants shall possess the gate of their enemies. In your seed all the nations of the earth shall be blessed, because you have obeyed My voice." So Abraham returned to his young men, and they rose and went together to Beersheba; and Abraham dwelt at Beersheba.

What you just read is Abraham getting ready to sacrifice his son without knowing that God would stop him. If you remember when Abraham got to the mountain he told the young men that he and his son would be back once again without knowing that God would stop him. That's faith. I say all this to say that what this scripture displays is faith, obedience, and the exact example of how we should be. I can't say what the future holds but I am pushing every day to not repeat any past patterns or to not let any distractions come my way to fall into the devils traps.

Be aware of your surroundings and if anything seems like a familiar pattern please go the other way. Don't feel bad about hurting someone's feelings if they don't get your number. They say they want to be your friend but it's a lie. They say they want to get to know you but that's only to figure out your vulnerability so they can "comfort" you. Don't be so quick to trust people or be happy about the first compliment you get.

If someone says you are beautiful just say thank you and keep going because you should know that already. The male gender studies the female gender and when they figure out your characteristics and actions then they have a hold on how to deal with you. Don't give them the satisfaction of giving the mysteries your husband should only unfold.

When your husband comes you will know because he will not only be a respectful gentlemen but he won't want anything from you but to be that man who compliments you. He will love your imperfections and won't embarrass you about them. He will be a listening ear and just know the right words without you explaining what you need him to say. This man will not be the type you are usually attracted to because that's your pattern and that's where the enemy waits. This man is molded by God specifically for you, will love you with the same love God does, and if you wait he will come. That's celibacy.

I thank God that I didn't have to go to rehab like my father and He called me in time for me to know the difference between the control of my actions. I'm not sure if my father knew any of this or even knew Christ but if I could've shared what I know now I would.

As I grow in this walk I learn more and more that I'm not in control. My mistake was thinking that once I've read my word I can stop for a couple of days or weeks and I'd be fine. Understand that your spirit has to continuously be fed by the word and if it's not then you will be tempted and fail. When I put my word down the first way the devil tempted me was sex and I failed every time. The spiritual battle is no joke.

When God finds you understand that your patience and strength will be tested but I'd rather have God test me then to have the devil keep a hold of me. If you think Christianity is too hard, think again, because this is the only faith that will test you to make you stronger and convict you when you're making the wrong decisions. I'm giving you the above information not to speak bad about anyone because trust I am not perfect but I need you to be aware of the devils tricks.

Giving your life to Christ means you are under the protection of God's unchanging hand. It means that you accept Jesus and all He has done for you. The most important thing is that you get to sit back and let the Lord fight your battles. You no longer have to carry the worries you normally would or figure out this and that on your own. When you are obedient to the Lord, which means doing what he asks of us in his word, then God will take care of His children. God is a big God and once you get to know him more and more your mind will expand to the depths of his glory to see just how great He is.

God is a deliverer but in order to be delivered from anything we have to want to live better. It all starts with the mindset and accepting salvation.

Romans 10:9-10 states: if you confess with your mouth the Lord Jesus and believe in your heart that God has raised Him from the dead, you will be saved. For with the heart one believes unto righteousness, and with the mouth confession is made unto salvation.

Romans 12:1-2 says: I beseech you therefore, brethren, by the mercies of God, that you present your bodies a living sacrifice, holy, acceptable to God, which is your reasonable service. And do not be conformed to this world, but be transformed by the renewing of your mind, that you may prove what is that good and acceptable and perfect will of God.

Both of these scriptures does two things: First, by confessing that Jesus is your Lord and Savior you are showing God that you accept His son in your life and you believe that he died on the cross for all of your sins including the ones you haven't committed yet. Second, you are acknowledging the steps you have to take

to build a relationship with the Lord and allowing Him to use you which you're experiencing an example of that right now reading this book. This is how God is using me. He told me that my purpose in life is to speak to females and to let them know that they are not alone. The hurt, the pain, secrecy, the brokenness is all the same feelings I felt but I had to be delivered from them in order to help other people through theirs.

Deliverance is more than being tired of your actions because you can easily go back to them, but deliverance is making a full lifestyle change to making better decisions all around. This could mean separating from the people who influence you, surrounding yourself with positivity and wisdom, and making a conscious effort every day to pray and read God's Word.

All of these drastic decisions will be easy for some but others like me it'll take a little longer to completely change your surroundings to make better decisions for your life. I had this problem because once I made the decision to follow Christ; the devil didn't want me to do right. He continued to use people from my past to cross my new path to get in my head to make bad decisions.

In the beginning you are weak so the more you fall and get up, the more you grow stronger and wiser to understand the proper steps to take the next time. It took me about two years to really get it right in my mind that I don't want to live a life of lust and fornication.

Now, I have no desire to have sex. I still get urges but I can't fathom going through the mental torment that sex brings me. *Hebrews 13:4 says Marriage is honorable among all, and the bed undefiled; but fornicators and adulterers God will judge.* The scripture is saying that when a married couple has sex their bed is not dirty but anyone else's bed is left dirty.

I have felt so filthy plenty of times and I knew once I realized that God was so displeased with me I had to change my life around even after my walk with Christ. I know you may be thinking, "Aren't you a Christian, you're not supposed to have sex?" My answer to you is demons attack Christians harder when the decision is made to follow Christ so I'm sorry but yes we mess up as well but this is why we follow the scripture *Acts 2:38*. It says, *"Then Peter said to them, "Repent and let every one of you be baptized in the name of Jesus Christ for the remission of sins; and you shall receive the gift of the Holy Spirit."*

When I repented for all of the filthiness my body endured, God heard me and cleansed me of it. He wrapped his arms around me and loved me with the unconditional love He has for his children. *John 3:16* says, *"For God so loved the world that He gave His only begotten Son, that whoever believe in Him should not perish but have eternal life."* I want eternal life so confessing, repenting, and transformation of the mind is what God instructs to get there.

Through this you have now shown Him that you want to live in the will or plan he has for your life. God loves us enough to watch us sin and go through the process of it because he knows we will be strengthened and our love for Him will grow. All God wants is for us to love Him back, to love our brethren, and to know in our minds that he is always with us.

1 John 4:7-21 says: Beloved let us love one another, for love is of God, and everyone who loves is born of God and knows God. He who does not love does not know God for God is love. In this love the love of God was manifested toward us, that God has sent His only begotten Son into the world that we might live through Him. In this is love, not that we loved God, but that He loved us and send His Son to be the propitiation for our sins. Beloved, if God so loved us we also ought to love one another. No one has seen God at any time. If we love one another, God abides in us, and His love has been perfected in us. By this we know that we abide in Him, and He in us, because He has given us of His Spirit. And we have seen and testify that the Father has sent the Son as Savior of the world. Whoever confesses that Jesus is the Son of God, God abides in him, and he in God. And we have known and believed the love that God has for us. God is love, and he who abides in love abides in God and God in him. Love has been perfected among us in this: that we may have boldness in the Day of Judgment; because as He is, so are we in this world. There is no fear in love; but perfect love casts out fear, because fear involves torment. But he who fears has not been made perfect in love. We love Him because He first loved us. If someone say, "I love God." And hates his brother, he is a liar, for he who does not love his brother who he has seen, how can he love God who he has not seen? And his commandment we have from Him: that he who loves God must love his brother also.

Love is important to God because he loves us. You might think that everything I'm explaining to you is difficult but it's actually as easy as confessing with your mouth and crying out to God that you want better. When you want better you do better. I had to cry out to God with a desperate cry for Him to change me. I couldn't do it on my own because it didn't work thus far. I needed help and God helped me. He heard my cry and comforted me with so much peace. Understand that God will do his part but you have to do yours. God will cleanse you but you,have to stay cleansed which is what I've been repeating over and over in the book; read your word. I stress this because in the book of Matthew it gives specific instructions on the way demons move:

Matthew 12:43-45: "When an unclean spirit goes out of man, he goes through dry places, seeking rest, and finds none. "Then he says, "I will return to my house from which I came, he finds it empty, swept, and put in order. "Then he goes and takes with him seven other spirits more wicked than himself, and they enter and dwell there; and the last state of that man is worse than the first. So shall it also be with this wicked generation."

Doesn't this scripture sound like my battles? My battles elevated because I kept putting my word down and more demons kept coming into my empty spirit. We have to feed the spirit so it can always be full so demons won't fit. We are stronger then Satan but we need God to defeat him on a daily basis.

Joyous Woman
11/11/2014

She looks over the mountain and sees nothing
Beautiful bright clouds, blue sky, and summer breeze blew
through her hair
Her vision is interrupted with tear drops because the wisdom she
possess knows it's something on the other side but she can't see it
The more she squints the smaller her site gets until her eyes are
fully closed
She starts to pray
As she wept the Lord gave her a sense of peace
and it finally hit her
The only way to seek the unknown is to seek the unknown
She starts to worship and God slowly expands her spiritual eyes
and clears the fog
Beauty is all she saw
The creation of God was more amazing then a pretty bird or the
sweetest song
Joy soared through her body, it was like she was lifted off the
ground weightless
Her worship grew and at this moment God knew she was ready
to fully surrender
She found triumph pushing through her doubts, her thoughts,
and her worries
Her strength was her direction but worship was the
breakthrough to the other side
And ever since that day her life was never the same
Through God she found glee which is why she made up in her
mind that she will forever praise his name

*I*n church I experienced how to praise and worship God which is another way of showing Him that you love Him. Praise is rejoicing in gladness that you are blessed and worship is the deep connection you and God are experiencing at that moment while in song or prayer. I love God so much that anytime I show Him gratitude I find myself worshipping more. I just really appreciate the life I have now and it's so awesome to know that He knew I would be here before I even knew.

The poem, "Joyous Woman" is a woman of freedom through salvation. She is the exact description of my inner joy and the peace that I endure in my life now. Christianity is my lifestyle. It isn't a hobby that I put down after I leave the church building. Being a joyous woman means I can show people what joy and freedom looks like because people especially God's queens need to know how good God is. I talk a lot of prayer and the importance of it but haven't explained why it is. Prayer is the direct conversation with God that explains our gratitude, request, cry, and warfare.

Prayer petitions God to answer the desire of our heart because He is our Father and will do anything for His child. You are a child of God just like I am and just a simple conversation will show you that He hears you and wants to talk to you to. To some that might sound weird because God is spirit but look at the many different emotions we have that we can't see but we can feel. Why not want to feel God when you know He will do no harm to you but love you? He gave me that dream when he said "come" because He wanted me to hurt no more. He wants you to be free to. Some of you might ask, "Brittany, how do you know all of this?" As I stated in the beginning, I don't have any credentials or a church title so to the church community I would not be qualified to give any of this information. But, God is my teacher and I know Him so well that no one can take away the gift I have to tell me that I'm wrong except for God.

God himself gives me so much wisdom and He is not shy of letting me know that He loves me. I read my word and I'm not shy about spreading the gospel. God specifically crafts our purpose to fit who we are and will become so as a person with a huge heart and no fear I guess I was the one of many who is supposed to speak this message. As you see throughout this book God gives me a lot of dreams as well.

Some are for comfort for me to know that He is with me and some are prophetic. I am not a prophet which is specific words from the Lord to give to his children to warn them or help them in their journey. I know one would say that sounds like your dreams and I would agree which why I said I'm prophetic. I am not a prophet because that is not God's plan for my life. My purpose as I said is to speak to the female reading this book and let her know that I know.

You think nobody knows but I do. I understand how it feels to be so deep in a hole and you're trying to get out but no one is rescuing you. I know what it feels like to feel alive and then want to die the next moment. I understand darkness and understand that I was comfortable there for a while until I was by myself with nothing around me but life. I wasted my life searching for love when I could've had it a long time ago.

Trust me I didn't ask for this. I didn't ask to be a Christian or even want to know who God was but it was time for me to stop dying. I just wanted to be free. Understand that the name Queen Freedom is not just a name it's my life. I'm not only a queen but I am free.

I wrote this book because I wanted to finally be free from anything people didn't know. I didn't want to have any secrets anymore even though people didn't know it was a secret. Somebody is going to read this book and say I can do it because Queen Freedom did it. I am no longer in bondage and Queen you don't have to be in bondage anymore either. I'm still standing, I'm still here, and God is continuing to strengthen me to tell my story. Every day the devil fights to keep me quiet but I refuse. I will not let any demon hide on my watch.

1 Peter 2:9-10 "But you are a chosen generation, a royal priesthood, a holy nation. His own special people, that you may proclaim the praises of Him who called you out of darkness into his marvelous light; who once were not a people but are now the people of God, who had not obtained mercy but now have obtained mercy."

Part 6:

Be Free Queen

Psalm 139:14
I praise thee that I am fearfully and
wonderfully made
Marvelous are thy works and my soul
knoweth right well

Single

*A girls dream is to get married, have a lavish life, white picket
house, and a fairy tale husband*
*One maybe two kids to become great success stories so when
they get old they can take care of you*
*You would think your agenda for your lifeline would plan out
smooth, but then life happens and you realize*
Before the marriage, the ring, the kids, your main goals
Before the moment he gets one his knee and propose
You're dying inside
Marriage and a baby won't keep him around
*When your life started with emptiness and although you've done
some nice patchwork*
Band aids get old and eventually expose the real reason you hurt
Quick to want someone to love, embrace, and adore you
*Quick to run in a relationship just for him to tell you you're
beautiful*
*But don't you know whether your light or dark skinned, small or
full figured you're beautiful*
*Your divine, elegant, gorgeous, enticing, angelic imperfections
are what make you beautiful*
*Maybe something's happened in your past that caused you to
have low self esteem*
*Maybe you were raised by your mom and your dad was a crack
head like me*
But you control your destiny
*And although life was hard your born again your past is gone
now your father is God*
Self-evaluate to predestinate your destiny
Deliverance speaks peace, freedom
Turns sympathy to empathy
*Throws confidence in the face of the enemy and pulls out the ugly
from deep within leaving nothing but the contents of your beauty*
The people that hurt you in your past

Whether you grew up with no mom or no dad is irrelevant
Because the God within will squeeze out of your temple and all
they can say is," It's something different about you"
You're the bone of bones
And flesh of flesh of a creation the Lord has made for his princess
But you have to endure the process
And know that a single mind is only a single time to get ready for
a single union with God
to elevate the covenant for two separate beings to become one
single climb
So for a single time
Seek His face in the midst of your wilderness
Because you have to fix you on the inside in order to love and to
be loved

I want you to know that God loves you not because he needs to but because he specifically chose us to be his people. You are special so walk in that.

Queens, if my testimony is yours I have only one answer for you, listen to your instinct because your instinct is your discernment. People like me second guess themselves and then double second guess themselves and still go with the wrong answer. What God does in my life is make those second and third guesses disappear by being the only answer I listen to. He gives clear instruction on the way we should go.

Keep this in mind, not everyone believes in God or even Jesus Christ, and that's ok, just understand you have to be free. Bondage is not an option. I was on Satan's side my whole life, dealing with the wrong people and becoming the monster my parents did not raise me to be. I hurt so many hearts and was so cold about it. Yes I was molested and my father was on drugs but it gets to a point where repetitious self-pain doesn't work when you use that excuse to cover your actions. Why I had these is because I had to think back to 6 years old when I was molested to understand why I'm so sexual. Then I had to remember how I felt when my father left to understand why I have abandonment issues and why I wanted the attention from a boy so bad. I wanted to be wanted by someone who I knew will never want me.

I was a person who always felt like a failure because in my mind nothing good was solid in my life. I had no legit foundation that I could stand on because I felt like I was just existing and not living. I never got good grades in high school or made any list of achievement. I continuously had to go to summer school because my grades were so bad. I was never motivated and had no drive because I was empty inside. I didn't have a purpose and had no clue what I wanted in life. All

I knew was sex. Nobody knew I cried at night for so many years because I hurt so bad inside. Nobody knew of the countless times I tried to commit suicide. Nobody knew the level of pain that elevated within me because of the questions that I had no answers to. Nobody knew how stupid I felt when I didn't walk across the stage with my class in high school because I once again failed another class. I constantly beat in my head that I was not good enough and no matter how much I tried that I would still be nobody. Nobody knew.

Queens when you suppress your anger so deep that you don't even know why you do things like have sex, this is when you should look in the mirror and see who you have become. Would the little girl in you like who you are? From the age of an infant to 5 years old is where I was the purest. I look back at her and remember her happiness, her love, and worth. From 6 years old on up I wasn't her anymore on the inside. We all have our pure age, think back to her and understand that you're still her.

Every day of this thing called life is not easy and we have to accept what we deserve not what we want for the moment. The only way we will accept what we deserve is to open those suppressed feelings and deal with it. We can't run, why, because like I said earlier if you're anything like me then you battle with evil thoughts and not getting any sleep just for a thought is draining.

I challenge you to do this: Every time you are mad, sad, lustful, etc. write down your thoughts you are experiencing through those feelings. Write down the justification of why this act is ok or what someone said to change your mind. Put it to the side and then read it when you have calmed down emotionally and sexually. Some people might just read it and have no reaction and others may read it and see an unrecognizable person. This friend is called a spirit, an entity that is not you. This is how you know it is time to make a change and get help. Look at yourself in the mirror every day and say one positive thing about you. It could be something as simple as, "You look beautiful today or (your name here) we will get through this day together. "Or simple say, "Yes you can" over and over again until you feel it. Speak your freedom every day and if you don't believe it then understand that you eventually will because your desire is to be free. Think about when you are at the gym at and you start to work out. When you proceed in doing your arm or leg reps you don't feel the burn until you do it about 10 or more times.

Encouraging yourself is that same way. When you look in that mirror to encourage yourself you might not feel it in the beginning but continue to declare that you will make it and you will eventually start to feel what you are repeating. Now that you have encouraged yourself, your mind will stay on that road to positivity because now you have spoken your freedom into existence.

When you get upset try your best to counter that with something positive. I personally love to color, sing, write, and dance. If you love to draw, paint, box, etc. make it your business to do that in the midst of your anger. Understand that when you get the hang of not giving into that anger you will realize your strength. Get "I can't " out of your head because then you won't.

Do you understand that you are a woman? We are borderline superheroes. I say that jokingly but the reason that a man cannot live without us is because we hold a big piece of the pie that he needs to get full. If you remember the story of Adam and Eve, the way God created Eve was from Adams rib. I'm not sure if you realize but without the rib a person cannot stand up straight or function. We are the strength that holds that man up straight. Aside from who we are to men, we have an inner strength that one can't imagine. I know you know that strength because you have gone through so much pain that the only way you are still going is strength.

Queen you are a pearl. Notice I did not say diamond because diamonds are hand made by man. Pearls are crafted in the sea and created by nature. The only way anyone can get to a pearl is if they dive in the sea to the bottom and grab the clam to retrieve the pearl. As far as sex, masturbation, and pornography it'll be trickier to counter because the urge is intense for a little while. But, it's the same strategy. Find something that will distract you from that feeling and go forth. Develop the mindset that your vagina is that pearl and if a man loves you enough he will marry to dive in that sea and retrieve your gem.

Love you and work on you. Don't give yourself to someone when you are broken because no matter how hard they try their love will never be enough. We don't want to be by ourselves because we'd rather not deal with our feelings so we'll get into long term relationships to cater to someone else's needs. The bad thing about that is this; ten years has gone by and you're still broken. When will you work on you? Start now and don't waste another second on him or them. Trust me I know it's HARD, I've failed more times than I've passed but I won't give up, I won't. I've hated myself to, I've harmed myself to, I've even hurt those around me but it gets to a point where it's exhausting being angry all the time.

Freedom isn't somebody you can call to say, "Hey, can I get a little freedom today." No! It is a lifestyle that you live; it is not a hobby that you pick up for convenience. How do you get freedom? I'm glad you asked. It starts from within. When you are at the point where you are desperate for a way out, that's when you are ready. Freedom is not something temporary just because you don't feel good about you because of your actions. Freedom wants a better way so those actions no longer have a chance to exist. God shows you a new way but first you have to accept salvation. As I stated earlier, this is accepting His son Jesus Christ as your Lord and Savior because you are acknowledging that He gave you the freedom that God will give you. The reason why you have the choice to be free is because

Jesus died for your sins to be forgiven on the cross. God had you, His child, in mind when Jesus had the assignment of crucifixion. Do you see Queen? You're special. God wants nothing more than to give you the desire of your heart but salvation is the first step.

If you want to make the decision to accept salvation in your life then here is how:

Romans 10:9-10: "If you confess with your mouth the Lord Jesus and believe in your heart that God has raised Him from the dead, you will be saved. For with the heart one believes unto righteousness, and with the mouth confession is made unto salvation."

Freedom means the chains are broken. Freedom is letting go of what you can't control. Freedom is taking your life back because your parent's issues have nothing to do with your life. It is waking up every morning refreshed because you have no worries in the world. Freedom knows that you are beautiful in spite of inner flaws. It is detaching from the negative and only looking at the positive because you know that God will carry the negative for you. It knows that you are not in control and believing in a higher power who is, God.

Freedom is walking with authority and teaching others how to do the same. It is grasping the ways of your inner thoughts and understands how to turn those thoughts to a positive. It is getting to know yourself so you know what areas to work on. Freedom is constantly sculpting your inner man and letting the hard layers peel so your heart can show through. It is trusting that God is guarding your heart so you can freely treat others with the love God allows you to show. Freedom knows how to encourage when you are having a rough day. It is the mindset of no matter what you will have joy. That's freedom, that is who I am, and I wear that name proudly.

Once I fully grasped this mindset I became a different woman. I didn't tolerate what the old me would have. I started to stand up for myself and use the word NO often. I began to love myself and I vowed that I would make sure I am treated with the love and respect I deserved. In every relationship I didn't care about me because it was all about them. Not anymore. God is first then me. I started to hang out with likeminded people who would encourage me while I was coming out of my old man. I didn't know how to operate in this new person I became so I couldn't be around the same folks. I even listen to different music now.

When you grow and develop into womanhood no matter the age, your surroundings will change as well as the things you do in your personal time. Little things like watching TV is something I've cut back on because I have things to do. I need to make sure I'm in the right headspace to move through life and I can't do that watching other people work. If you've noticed, television is nothing more than watching other people do their jobs and I was sitting on the couch watching them. No. Fill your time with school, work, hobbies, ministry, giving back, etc.

Basically, anything that makes you a better woman inside and out. Learn how to do something if you have no interests until something sticks. Don't just exist in this world but be somebody great. Let people know you for your accomplishments and not for your battles. Understand that after reading this book, people will know both all wrapped in one because my story is how I survived. I'm a warrior and know that you are as well.

My scars will never define me but they are the reason why I'm here and the reason why I'm free. I don't know why God chose me to go through but I did and endured. Queen, you have to know that you can to. Just imagine how screwed up in the head I was and now I can speak freedom to other Queens. That's nothing but God, I don't care what anyone says. I could've been in rehab like my father, in a psychiatric institute, in jail, or even worse dead but I'm here.

The reason why I can love people how I do is because I make sure my joy is solid. I can't encourage anybody if I am drained and unhappy all the time. I do this by making sure I have quiet time for myself and with God. I write, sing, or whatever it takes to get all frustration out. I will not carry any emotional baggage in my quiet time or with my time with God because my mind won't be fully there. You'd be surprised at how many people you hold a conversation with and they are not fully there. It's because they aren't free. Be free Queen, and teach other queens to do the same. It'll change your life and theirs to. I call females queens because that is literally who you are; royalty. You are the daughter of a King and you need to know that God loves his little girls. Every time I see a queen I make sure I call her who she is because if she hears it enough, she will start believing it to be true.

I want to leave you with the following poem because I understand you think nobody gets you but if you don't remember one thing from this book understand that I know. I have felt the deepest amount of anger one body can feel. It was so enormous that I didn't want to continue my walk with God but just know that He sends us through that pain to be a testimony to someone else. So with these final words I want you to know that I love you and this book was not easy for me to write. I was embarrassed and I'm also not the best "professional" writer using big and fancy words but I will do it over and over again for you. All of my secrets are on the table. Wait on the Lord, why, because if he can change my filthiness then he can certainly turn it around for you. What is the Art of Salvation?

It's Freedom

God Bless

My Vow

I am you and you are me
I hated myself, I thought I was ugly
Suicide attempts and homicidal thoughts
Filled my brain while my body rots

Sex was all I ever had
Comparing to my inner sad
Drugs was like a fairy tale
To visit the land where I could dwell

My heart was black, my body cold
My love was never a prize to hold
I gave my body, I sold my soul
But God took back what Satan stole

I am you and you are me
God turned the hate and loved the ugly
He is all you'll ever need
To find joy and inner peace

My vow to you is not a lie
My vow is all I have inside
You may still hurt and want to die
My vow is truth so you will rise

A Message to my Mother

I understand you because I am you. You are my hero not only because you are a tremendously strong woman but through that you taught my sister and I the core value of the importance of family. I understand why we went through what this book explains with my dad because you have the same story as I do. The difference between who I am now and who you were when you were my age is freedom. God has restored me of any pain that I ever felt growing up and he can do the same for you to. You don't have to be secret anymore. You have to go back to when you were a child and remember it all. Let yourself feel those emotions and just cry. Let the tears flow. Call out to God and surrender to Him. He will take every single burden you have right now.

Don't be afraid of what others think because other opinions should never affect you. I declare that as we take this journey together, those opinions will bounce off of your shoulders. The devil will no longer keep you in bondage and know that your mind is so precious to God. Give Him your all and know that you can come to me for anything. I will pray with you, laugh with you, cry with you, and listen to you until freedom becomes the only thing you speak out of your mouth. God called me out of darkness first so you can see what freedom looks like. I am the light in the house and if you haven't realized yet you are my ministry.

I began this message by saying, "I understand you because I am you." This statement is the truest thing I've ever said to you. I know you don't fully understand me but as you let God control those things you control now, you will start to understand me. You are so strong and know that if you haven't

109

broken yet from those trials then its more fire in you then you even know.

Remember I was a little timid shy girl who wouldn't hurt a fly but now I'm a prayer warrior and God can use me because He knows I will fight until the end. It's time for you to love yourself and allow you to have joy. You've given your life to your kids and you lost yourself. Spend every day getting to know you all over again and fall in love with all of you. You'll find some things you don't like because you'll see them in your kids and that's when you'll start to begin your freedom journey.

Free the inner her who won't speak. I guarantee those shackles will break and it'll feel so liberating. Some time ago God told me that even though you are my mother I have to look at you as a broken woman first because that way I won't expect you live up to a title that looks like perfection in my eyes. After that day I saw you in a different light. Mom you are just like me which means that those chains will break because I'm living it on the other side. Gods' arms are open and waiting for you because it's your turn now.

SPEAK YOUR FREEDOM

About the Author

Brittany "Queen Freedom" Williams is a domestic and sexual abuse survivor and only through God has she had the courage to break free and help others in their situations through her transparency. Brittany states, "Queen Freedom" is the name God gave her to show women through her own imperfections that a queen comes from within. She has been a writer, singer, and liturgical dancer from a very young age and continues to use her gifts and talents to inspire the world. She has ministered poetry throughout the DMV area including group homes and shelters as well as the Philadelphia area just to name a few. Queens Freedom's testimony is also a part of the book, "Moments in her story: Second Edition". This is a book of testimonies written by amazing women like Queen Freedom and young adult females who have a story to tell and want to inspire and encourage people like you. Brittany also instructs female only Shut In's four times a year called, "Speak your Freedom". It is an overnight scripture based getaway that for females who need an outlet to come together to be transparent and confident with their thoughts, emotions, questions, fears, and baggage. Through numerous topics she is able to uncover deeply rooted issues that need to be addressed to break any forms of bondage. Queen Freedom's passion to uplift females like her gives her the liberation to know that one by one females are being healed through Christ. She always states, "My ministry is not for everybody but for the female who feels like she has nobody." Queen Freedom is a woman with a humble heart, a mind to serve, and an inner boldness that only through God has she been able to live up to being called Queen.

The Art of Salvation

10/08/2013

There once was a blank canvas that
sits on the arms of wood stand
And as lonely as it is, it can't get to its fullest potential without
the touch of its creator's hands
So it sits and it waits for the masterpiece to start
And every imperfection that empty canvas experiences doesn't
matter because in the end they are one
See the Lord says to be still and he will come to give you the next
color on the paint brush
And smoothly paint the bright colors of joy over the dark ruins of
your life that it tries to rush
See salvation will allow you to separate from the flesh in this life
And God will fully map it out and salvage any brush strokes that
fell off course in your next life
See we can't turn our back on God because he loves us
We have to look inside to find him and ground yourself in the
Word all day and all night if you have to
See these black Hitler's kill us mentally, that's why God has to
intercede and be our median
But to many people laughed at Jesus as he teach the word but
when he rose on the third day
they found out he was no comedian
See we have to spend time in the mirror, because Jesus doesn't
want us to see through
Our reflection is his reflection on our reflection which is the
Spirit in him
We have to transform to the Spirit and not conform to the flesh
Because we have to be in position for the Lord
to prepare you for your purpose
See I think that were too comfortable in the ship

We get scared by the noisy storms and winds around us
But salvation will allow you to stay focused on that light without
questioning in your mind if you think that it's Jesus
But see people lost hope in Peter because as he began to sink his
faith turned into fear
But the most important part that people miss is
Jesus didn't leave him sinking
He lift him up from below, But below will keep you sunk in until
you decide to throw your hands up and surrender your flesh so
your Spirit can begin
See God loves you, He loves you, He loves you
Even after we committed the worst sin
And after we have the audacity to sin again
The Lord still blocks the evil that comes your way and says,
"You better not touch this child who worked
so hard to get into this kingdom"
But this only happens when we renew our minds and wait for our
creator to fulfill our hearts
But to be like that blank canvas that waits for its creator that I
mentioned from the start
We have to look up, outside, and inside ourselves for our
masterpiece of art